Nfl Football

Understand the Rules and Positions in Nfl Football

(Basic Knowledge of Nfl Football History With Some Fun Facts and Records)

Mario Doty

Published By **Ryan Princeton**

Mario Doty

All Rights Reserved

Nfl Football: Understand the Rules and Positions in Nfl Football (Basic Knowledge of Nfl Football History With Some Fun Facts and Records)

ISBN 978-1-77485-894-3

ISBN 978-1-77485-894-3

Legal & Disclaimer

The information contained in this ebook is not designed to replace or take the place of any form of medicine or professional medical advice. The information in this ebook has been provided for educational & entertainment purposes only.

The information contained in this book has been compiled from sources deemed reliable, and it is accurate to the best of the Author's knowledge; however, the Author cannot guarantee its accuracy and validity and cannot be held liable for any errors or omissions. Changes are periodically made to this book. You must consult your doctor or get professional medical advice before using any of the suggested remedies, techniques, or information in this book.

TABLE OF CONTENTS

Introduction

I grew up playing football.

I grew up with the sights and smells, the tears, the sweat your blood and the victories, and the loss. I was literally born on the field and found the passion and enthusiasm for the sport as I couldn't even get my eyes open.

I didn't grow up playing hockey.

I can remember every Thanksgiving my family would gather and watch a hockey match. No matter if I was 6, 8 or 10 I never found the rules much easier for me to comprehend. When my family was cheering on various players and different aspects of the game that I didn't even imagine, I was bored, uninterested, and possibly drank too of diet soda. It's impossible to know what's going on with the same thing when everyone other people are so involved.

This is the thing about football here in America that fans are extremely engaged. From outrageous outfits to stunning face paint and screaming to the roof of their voices for three hours It's clear: Americans love their football.

My aim for all of you reading this book is for you to be able to reach a level of fundamental football knowledge and also enjoyment.

Chapter 1: Birth Of A League

The very beginning of the NFL is quite remarkable that the league has survived for so long. There were ten groups across four states. Everyone was wearing a calfskin cap that they could tuck in and put in their pockets as well as establishments with names such as the Muncie Flyers and the Toledo Maroons really existed.

Humble Beginnings

If you've never heard about the Hupmobile then it's a good thing. The brand of automobile started in 1909, and was largely gone from the center of commerce until World War II. It was however at the Hupmobile showroom situated in a tiny town known as Canton, Ohio, that the NFL was first united. It was only the teams that were part of the Ohio League that first day when was the day that American Professional Football Conference was established. After one month, the organization was renamed as the American Professional Football Association, including Buffalo, Rochester, Detroit and Hammond being added to the mix along with other groups. The first eleven clubs put up a rule that said they would not be taking players from one another (a training session was turned into poaching later in the early hours) and would declare a winner at the end of the season.

The president of the association of the association was American famous Jim Thorpe, who was active at the time. The first season, 1920, was filled with planning issues and hiccups however only four of the 11 groups finished their season, including one group, the Akron Pros named association champions. The following year, membership increased to 22 groups and the majority of newbies out of New York State. Two groups from that year remain within the organization. There is the Decatur Staleys ultimately turned into the Chicago Bears, while the Chicago Cardinals at last moved to St. Louis and afterward out west towards Arizona. As baseball fought to allow dark players throughout the final period of the 1940s, the NFL initially allowed the players to play. However, they it stopped the training in 1927. It took nearly twenty years before being reintegrated. The league was close to changing two times prior to the 1910s. In the first instance was halted by the US"section" of World War I. The next time, the influenza pandemic that began in 1918, and killed 3 to 5 percent of the population restricted travel for groups. In fact, 28 percent from the US portion of population was restricted from traveling in groups. In total, 28 percent out of US 675,000 people died.

Jim Thorpe

If Jim Thorpe were a youngster today, he'd have over 500 million fans on Twitter, earn $500 million annually in donations, and also have a news channel that is 24 hours a day dedicated solely to what he would accomplish. Thorpe was the unbeatable American rival in the days prior to the time when Babe Ruth began pummeling homers every day. A member of The Sac and Fox Nation, Thorpe was introduced to this world around 1887, in the area that is now Oklahoma. In 1904, aged 16 years old, Thorpe attended Carlisle Indian Industrial School and was instructed by the legendary GlennScobey "Pop" Warner. He was a player in football and baseball, as well as lacrosse and of course the universally loved game formal dancing. In fact, he was awarded the intercollegiate 1912 title. Incredibly, Warner did not need to play football because he was stupefying in the track. When he was at Carlisle College, he played running back, defensive back, placekicker and punter. He scored his entire team's goals in a rout of 18-15 of Harvard's No. 1 Harvard. in 1912 Carlisle took home the title public when Thorpe ran for 1,869 yards in 191 conveys. He scored 25 points. Thorpe also competed during the 1912 Summer Olympics in the pentathlon and decathlon and won gold on two times and winning eight out of fifteen competitions throughout. He then played in a few periods in Major League Baseball with the New York Giants, Cincinnati Reds as well as the Boston Braves over the course of the next few years, and then returned to his initial fascination with football. He signed a contract with his team the Canton Bulldogs in 1915 for the huge sum of $250 per game and the number of players in the group grew from 1,200 to 8,000 every game. Canton was awarded the title of association during 1916, 1917 and 1919. Then, it joined in the APFA in 1920, with Thorpe as its president. He played until he was 41, and had played 52 NFL games with six teams from 1920 to 1928.

Green Bay Packers

There was a semipro organization located in Green Bay, Wisconsin, from 1896 onwards and Earl Lambeau and George not decided to adhere to the same model during the latter part into the decade 1910. Lambeau and Calhoun were adversaries on the football field at secondary school but they subsequently teamed up to get an extraordinary thing moving. Lambeau was the leader of the Green Bay East High's sports team and also its captain in 1917. He was a player in 1918 and was a player in the team of Knute Rockne in Notre Dame. The team was formed in 1919, but didn't form any players until 1920. The team and then joined the newly created NFL on the 27th of August 1921. They've been playing in the NFL continuously since then, making it the longest consecutive time in the organization. Within their first decade on the field, Packers became the top team of the organization. In 1927, they were 7-2-1 under Lambeau's guidance as a coach and player. The New York Giants (11-1-1) were more successful.

They scored 12-0-1 in 1929, and beat eight of their 13 rivals. In the whole season they only allowed 22 focuses, which included three scores and a few protections. In the standoff against lasting force New York, they destroyed the Giants 20-6.

They returned as champions of the association in the years 1930 and 1931 and they had their first harvest of Hall of Famers such as Mike Michalske, Johnny McNally, Carl Hubbard, and society saint Arnie Herber Arnie Herber, one of the Green Bay local. In the first season game, the Packers were able to win 29 straight home games which is a record that has not been broken.

The team finished the year with three consecutive shutouts and a massive throng of 20,000 fans embraced the team when they knocked off their biggest rival that is their rivals, the Chicago Bears, 25-0 to finish the season.

They were 10-3-1 in 1930, finishing simple rate focuses ahead of Giants (13-4) to win the title. They played a season-long game with New York and New York, taking 14-7 at home while losing 13-6 on the road. In 1931 the Packers became the primary group to take home three NFL championships in succession, after they finished the year with a 12-2-2 record. The closest competitor to their rivals, the Portsmouth

Spartans, who went 11-3. Overall the Packers won 11 titles between 1929-1967 , and would add 4 Super Bowl wins since.

The Title Dispute of 1925 Title Dispute

Six years into the evolution of the NFL the league was undergoing its first debate. Five new groups were incorporated into the league: the New York Giants, the Detroit Panthers, the Providence Steam Roller as well as the newly formed Canton Bulldogs, and the Pottsville Maroons.

The Maroons were a major success with six wins in their first seven games all with shutouts. Their biggest loss was defeat the Providence Steam Roller by a six-point advantage. Their remaining matches they won by a total result of 179-0.

Their most successful game of the season occurred on the 6th of December in which they defeated all of the Chicago Cardinals 21-7 out and around. The win could have earned Pottsville their first NFL title, but the following week, they scheduled an event to play with the University of Notre Dame All-Stars in Philadelphia and won 9-7. They Frankford Yellow Jackets played a game the same day in Philadelphia and complained to the association and complained to the association that Pottsville was in violation of regional rights. NFL President Joe Carr fined the club and later removed it from all rights and honors, including the possibility to compete to win the league title. The Cardinals played two more games, and finished being 11-2-1 and the Maroons at 10-2. In 2003 the NFL presented its owners with the idea of for a rerun of the case, but the league voted 30-2 in its favor and only Pottsville and two other Pennsylvania establishments, and the Steelers and Eagles casting votes for.

George Halas

Halas was always lucky from 1915 onwards, beginning when he ran late and was unable to board the SS Eastland, which went onto capsize and kill the 844 passengers. He was one of the co-founders of the NFL and later retired with the name "Mr. Everything." It's a small wonder that he co-founded and owned the Chicago Bears, played in the league as the radio's producer inventor and even an elite baseball player. He attended at the University of Illinois and played basketball, baseball and football with the Illini and earned an engineering diploma in civil engineering during his spare time . He also helped the team achieve in 1918 the Big Ten Conference title. He could have gone straight to professional after football, but instead he was an officer with the Navy during World War I where he was a member of the Great Lakes Naval Training Station. College teams were almost non-existent due to conflict and they agreed to play in the Pasadena Tournament of Roses agreedto an New Year's Day game in 1919, at the fifth Rose bowl, which featured players from Great Lakes Navy Bluejackets and the Mare Island Marines. Halas scored a touchdown of 32 yards passing in the 3rd quarter. He also recorded a 77-yard intercept return, a record that holds the record for the longest return of an interception that didn't result in a touchdown during Rose Bowl history. In recognition of his achievements that day, he was voted the winner of the game. When he left the Navy and playing minor-time baseball, weighing 12 games as an outfielder for 1919's New York Yankees, going 2 for 22 (.091) at the plate. His most famous partner may be the most important piece of baseball-related random data, Wally Pipp. A formidable first baseman Pipp became the Yankees regular first baseman between 1915 and.

The Yankees had a difficult time in 1925 and Pipp contributed to the problem batting .244 during 41 games. In the 15-26 group, the director decided to sit Pipp for one match in place of an unnamed tenderfoot Lou Gehrig. Gehrig scored a hit, and then on to the next game, followed by the next one, and the next. He was able to score twenty grand slams , and an average of RBI and hit .295 of each of his two

thirds of an entire season. Pipp did not get his spot back, but Gehrig played in record-breaking 2,130 consecutive games. Halas was not Gehrig but not as much as an Pipp but he did pass on baseball to join Hammond Pros. Hammond Pros, procuring $75 per game playing on the field.

A one year later He worked living in Decatur working for the starch producer the A.E. Staley Company, where he was involved in deals, played in the club's organization ball and also served as a mentor for the company's Decatur Staleys. He took his school's tones, naval force blue and orange--and transformed them into Staleys. In 1920, at just 25 years old He was the first to address his fellow Staleys at the well-known gathering that was the basis for the American

Professional Football Association in Canton. Two years later the association was transformed to the NFL.

In his first year as a mentor the Staleys had a 10-1-2 record, but they didn not draw crowds. The organizer of the organization gave the team to Halas who then moved the team to Chicago with the same name until 1921 when they were awarded the title of association. The title was a distorted one, given that Buffalo AllAmericans Buffalo AllAmericans had the best record (9-0-2) while Chicago finishing third (7-1-0). Both teams took part in the match that Buffalo intended to be an open-air game towards season's conclusion. Even though they lost, Buffalo still had the most impressive record, however Halas persuaded the two clubs, Canton and the Chicago Cardinals to end the year with more wins and win the title away from Buffalo.

The year 1922 was the time he changed the name of the Staleys in 1922 to in 1922, the Chicago Bears, an accolade for the town's renowned baseball team named the Cubs.

Halas not just claimed the team and directed the team, but the player also served as a as a wide beneficiary and guarded end. He was a member of his 1920's All NFL group, but his most remarkable moment was in 1923, when he took Jim Thorpe for a bumble and returned it 98 yards to score an impressive score. It was an unbeaten record that stood until 1972. The year 1925 saw him was selected by Red Grange to the Bears. He quit as a coach and player in the year 1930, but remained the owner and was back in training in 1933 in order to eliminate the cost of having a head trainer! He was a trainer for the next ten years, and introduced the scandalous offensive known as Wing-T during the final portion of the 1930s that was so brutal it enabled the Bears to set two standing records after they wiped out all of the Washington Redskins 73-0 in the 1940 NFL championship game.

1927 New York Giants

There aren't many groups that have had the same success as the 1927 Giants were able to do. The season was triggered by an extraordinary gathering that dismantled with less shaky groups, mainly located in the Midwest and placed higher top players on fewer dreams. The association was reduced to twelve groups, and the NFL increased its presence on its East Coast, remembering two groups from New York City: Red Grange's Yankees and their rivals The New York Giants. The Giants had been 8-4-1 in the previous year and finished 6thplace, but had solved the issue in the following year, winning their final four games, and all by shutout. They had worked it out afterward, and won their final four games, and all by shutout. The team was 0-1, with wins of 8-0 over Providence as well as a 0-0 tie with Cleveland and a 19-0 triumph against Pottsville. Their first loss was only a minor one, a 6-0 loss to Cleveland but they scored five consecutive shutouts over 17 days.

They showed their humanity by allowing scores to Cardinals as well as the Bears in their 28-7 and 13-7 victories, and then sweeping the Yankees twice, 14-0 and 13-0 in order to claim the title of association champion. As their defensive abilities grew as did their popularity. Their popularity increased dramatically. Giants attracted 20,000 supporters to their triumph over Pottsville in the week of

7. Seven days after the event 38,000 people flocked on the Polo Grounds to watch them remove on the Steam Roller.

In the course of the season, the Giants finished 11-1-1 and outscored their opponents by 197-20. They also allowed 1.5 focus per game which was the lowest amount of focuses allowed ever during NFL history. They took the title of association by four games, beating Green Bay (7-2-1). Fullback Jack McBride scored 57 focuses for the team, squabbling for six points and kick 15 more focuses, and two field goals. The team was first placed after a lengthy period of time allowed and gained yards as well. Duke Potteiger was the head coach.

Joe Guyon

In another institution, the Joe Guyon could be a great teacher at any time. In the time it was time to Carlisle Indian Industrial School, Guyon was not the greatest player in his own class. It's because that Guyon was a student at the same time at the same school like Jim Thorpe, who many consider to be the most formidable athlete this country has had in the past. Guyon had a background as an American Indian from the Chippewa family and came into the world at White Earth, Minnesota. Similar to Thorpe the player was with Pop Warner, yet he was a left tackle and but not an elementback. The 1912 team was awe-inspiring by scoring 454 focuses and being 12-1-1. The group was playing against Army the team, which featured the future US Presidency Dwight D. Eisenhower and the first all-American in the group Leland DeVore, who could be the Army's first commander.

Officials from the engine transport. DeVore was so dissatisfied by Guyon the way he played that he kicked out of the game. The moment that Thorpe quit for his geniuses Guyon was named halfback. The team was 10-2-1. Guyon was selected as an all-American second-group player. He then played at Georgia Tech in 1917-1918 under an instructor named John Heisman, whose name is still echoed to this day. The team of 1917 was 9-0 and averaged 54.5 goals per game and for a long period afterwards, was considered "the most impressive team the South could offer at any time." Guyon was totally determined, with his initial performance of the game going 75 yards and scoring in the game against Wake Forest.

When Tech defeated Vanderbilt 83-0, Guyon sprinted several times to 344 yards. It was a staggering 29 yards per transfer, and against Tulane all of the four players in Georgia Tech's backfield went over 100 yards speeding. Guyon delivered two scores and ran for another.

The team of 1918 was less efficient as Guyon was split between halfback and tackle. In 1919, Guyon became master before joining with the Canton Bulldogs. From 1919 to the year 24 the two of them Thorpe played alongside one another before Guyon was able to join with the Kansas City Cowboys. Guyon was awarded a title by in 1927 with the New York Giants. In the time the team wasn't pounding mouths while playing, he would be working on the sidelines. He was a coach for his team of Union University Bulldogs in 1919 and returned at the school to teach the team for all games between 1923 and 27. He also taught students from the St. Xavier Secondary school located in Louisville, KY, from 1931 to 1933.

As his fellow American Indian star Thorpe, Guyon was a superb baseball player , hitting more than .340 for three consecutive years within the

American Association for the Louisville Colonels. Guyon was a good baseball trainer , also driving Clemson between 1928 and 31.

Jimmy Conzelman

There's nothing Jimmy Conzelman could not do to improve his performance. He was a remarkable player, a remarkable teacher as well as an extraordinary coach, Navy man as well as a baseball coach, and a master of publicizing. He was introduced to the world of St. Louis in 1898 He attended Loyola Academy and afterward Central High School. He began his career at Central High as a halfback and later moved into McKinley High after a redesign of the school, competing for the football field, basketball and track. He won the title of association as the quarterback in 1915.

He went through until Washington University in 1916, however, he was drafted into his first year in the US Navy the next year. Conzelman was the quarterback in the 1917 Great Lakes Navy Bluejackets group that hammered not only Navy that was undefeated until the point of this, but also The Mare Island Marines by a 17-0 win at the

1919 Rose Bowl. Amazingly, Conzelman was a close teammate of two other potential NFL lobby of famers from the group, namely Paddy Driscoll and George Halas.

Following the war after the war, he went back to school and led Washington to a 5-2 mark in 1919, as his team outscored rivals by 127-30. He was unable to play in the next year due to his academics and his stepfather was kicked out of the game and he was forced to leave school, he did so in large part to help his mother as well as younger sister and brothers.

As it was announced that the American Professional Football Association was created, he was once more involved and joined with the Decatur Staleys, the antecedent to the Chicago Bears. They were reunited there alongside his previous teammate George Halas. In his debut game, he scored the primary score on an impressive 43-yard run. He started as a halfback punter, punter, and placekicker as well as quarterback based on the circumstances. The Staleys were second in the league with a record of 10-1-1.

In the next year, he was a part of his fellow players in the Rock Island Independents as both the captain as well as a mentor. At the age of 23, he was possibly the youngest coach in NFL history , and he led the team to a 4-1 record. He continued coaching and playing in the following year for his team, the Milwaukee Badgers, driving them to a 7-2-3 win in 1923. He scored four goals and two more points.

In just about two years of his birth, he traded caps and become the owner of the NFL facility in Detroit that he named the Panthers. It cost him just $50 to acquire the business, which is about $700 at the moment in dollars. He wore the hats of owner, player and coach of the Panthers. The team was 8-2-2 and beat its opponents by 129-39. Participation increased dramatically in the next year as well, and Conzelman returned the group to the organization for $1200. Conzelman did have the pork skin in his veins in spite of that, and was accepted as a player, administrator as well as a mentor in that 1927 Providence Steam Roller. He scored four goals and helped the group achieve an 8-5-1 mark, and the following year brought Providence its first NFL title by winning 8-1-2. Conzelman was named the team MVP. In

21

1929, the group played 4-6-2, and Conzelman was hesitant to play.

He was able to mentor himself as well as in the school, before being able to be a mentor for in the Chicago Cardinals from 1940-1942. The game was far from an impressive game with the Cardinals, as the team finished just 8-22. He resigned from the NFL to become the chairman of the St. Louis Browns ball club in 1943. He was there for two years with the club's owner Donald Brown and saw the club be awarded an award from the American organization in 1944.

Conzelman returned to Cardinals Cardinals as a coach in 1946. The accomplishment came about at this time for Conzelman since the Cardinals were victorious in their 1947 NFL Championship game over the Philadelphia Eagles, and went 11-1 in 1948 before losing this title in the end in the hands of the Eagles. Conzelman was 26-9 over the following three seasons of the team. Conzelman sparked an interest in publicizing later in the future and, out of the blue, gave up after the second NFL championship game to take an opening at D'Arcy Advertising Co. He was a key figure in an NFL's 2nd Hall of Fame class in 1964.

In 1968, a monument to him was dedicated to Busch memorial Stadium situated in St. Louis.

He passed away in 1970 aged 72. In 2006 He was one of the eight contract participants from the Arizona Cardinals Ring of Honor.

Paddy Driscoll

There's not much greater Midwest soccer than John Leo"Paddy Driscoll." He was born to the world in Evanston, Illinois, and died in Chicago. He was a student at Northwestern and was a great player with Hammond, Racine, and Chicago. He was a trainer for the Bears exactly like Marquette University. Driscoll was just 143 pounds at the time of his school, but this didn't hinder his ability to be a courageous halfback. He scored nine points on a score as well as an objective on the field when Northwestern beat Chicago 10-0 in every game of 1916, when the Wildcats first triumphed over their rivals in fifteen years. He also played on team for baseball and ball.

He was indeed skilled enough to join The Chicago Cubs throughout the late spring of 1917. It was a brief review of the game, since Driscoll only played in thirteen games, hitting .107 with a double of three runs batted into and a few stolen bases.

The following fall when he was a member of in the Hammond Clays and right away transformed into a star leading the team to victory at the Indiana Championship. The all-rounder Driscoll was a massive success from the beginning of October 1917 and scoring each of the 20 Hammond's highlights (three scores, and two more focus) during a victory of 20-0 over Wabash. One of his scores was the opening shot returned for an unofficial score that began the second quarter from the last quarter. One of his strengths was his ability to punt the ball with incredible accuracy and distance. It was believed that he was the greatest drop kicker in the beginning of the era. He was the only player to score all of the team's goals again, before the 5,000 players to beat Pine Village 13-0. It was only the following unfortunate incident that Pine Village had

Experienced over twelve years.

Seven days after the event, Driscoll was thumped oblivious in the 2nd half against Cornell. He was able to return to the field in the final minute and kick an objective of 55 yards to secure 13-3. In the final quarter of the game the player scored three points and added a point in a win of 25-0 against Fort Wayne.

As a lot of his colleagues, Driscoll ended up in the Navy during World War II and played alongside George Halas and Jimmy Conzelman. Being a past brilliant footballer, Driscoll was denied the possibility of playing for his club, the Great Lakes Navy Bluejackets group. In the final decision, he was allowed to join the team and had the ball going in a 54-14 win of Rutgers when Driscoll ran for six scores and kicked five goals. In 1919's Rose Bowl, he punted on a field goal and made the ball to Halas who was likely to become a deeply rooted friend. The post-game report of 1919, The Los Angeles Times essayist said, "Driscoll needs no recognition. He's the most impressive backfield player we've any point anywhere in Southern California and had at his disposal a fine football team as anyone could wish for."

A few weeks after following the Rose Bowl win, he was traded with the Chicago Cubs to the Los Angeles Angels. He was ecstatically returned home to Southern California and played shortstop in the Pacific Coast League, hitting .264 with four triples, three copies and a home run.

In the fall of that year, he was a player with his team, the Hammond All-Stars alongside Halas. In the game at Wrigley Field, he returned an extra 50 yards of dropkick for an assist, then kicked field goals and another three points.

The following season, he was a part of his fellow players, the Racine Cardinals and was named the group's commander. In the first season of the NFL, he led the team achieve a 6-2 record. He returned to Wrigley field for a game against the Chicago Tigers. In front of 7,000 people they he scored a dropkick to score the winning goal with a 6-3 win. This wasn't the main event but his primary game victory against Decatur. The Cardinals finished 7-2-2 and fourth. Driscoll was named the first-team all-quarterback.

in 1921 Driscoll continued to be skipper, and a mentor in informal form. In a win of 20-0 over Minneapolis the following year, he ran for a point while throwing another and kicked two more goals. In November of that year, he hit a field goal of 35 yards with just four minutes left to create a 3-3 tie together with Green Bay Packers. Green Bay Packers. The Cardinals

The team climbed to third in 1922 with an record of 8-3. The teams got bigger as his fame grew. The Cardinals defeated the Bears twice in just three weeks prior to hordes of 10,000 and 12,000. The player scored three field objectives in the following success in a 9-0 slugfest. Driscoll led through the NFL with scoring goals in 1923. He had the setting up of 78 focus points in seven scoring points, 10 field goals as well as six additional focused. He scored 19 of these locations in a 19-0 win against Akron. In the first five games of that game the player scored 69 focus points before getting injured.

It was 1924 when Driscoll delivered a field target during the initial game of the season. The record was for 29 years.

The year was. The record was for 29 years.

2-1. Driscoll was once again the primary scorer of the team and scored 67 goals on 11 field targets as well as four scores. 10 other focus. In November of that year when the Cardinals faced their rivals, the Chicago Bears before a limit crowd of 36,000. It was the occasion to present Red Grange with the Bears However, Driscoll dropped the ball away from him which drew boos from the crowd. The Chicago Tribune applauded Driscoll for his actions, stating that the player was"out trying for the win, not to let Grange to organize the Roman celebration on their behalf."

The next season, Driscoll got a contract with the Bears and led them to an impressive 12-1-3 record. He recorded a career high of with 86 focuses, six scores and 12 field goals as well as 14 more focus. The 12 field goals beat his previous record. After completing his being trained at secondary school and at the school levels, Driscoll was recruited by his long-time friend George Halas as an associate coach for the Bears. He was there until the year 1955, when he won four NFL titles in a row. Then, in the year 1956, he was enlisted by Halas to replace him. He remained with the Bears at various positions until 1963, before choking the dust in the year 1968. Halas described Driscoll as "the greatest competitor I've ever met."

Guy Chamberlain

A remarkable player who transformed into a much more renowned mentor and the proud of Blue Springs, Nebraska, was among the most talented players at the start of NFL. He helped lead Nebraska's Nebraska Cornhuskers to numerous Missouri Valley Conference titles and in 1936, was named the most outstanding athlete in Nebraska history. He played in the top football leagues for a lengthy period with seven groups, and also won championships over six times in his 9 seasons. as a player with the 1919 Canton Bulldogs and the 1921 Chicago Staleys, and as an instructor in the 1922-1924 Bulldogs and for the 1926 Frankford Yellow Jackets.

In his six years as an instructor in the lead trainer position, he had his record to 58-16-7. This is the most impressive performance of any coach with at least 50 wins. He's also the principal coach who won the NFL title, with three distinct groups. He was initially a back, but the coach was promoted to end in 1915 and scored 15 points on passes. He led the Huskers to an incredible 20-19 win against Notre Dame and scored four scores in his final contest, 52-7 loss of Iowa. It is amazing that he was able to return to farming after graduation and joined serving in the Army during World War

II, positioned in Kentucky, Oklahoma, and San Diego.

He was back in football in 1919 and played with Jim Thorpe 's Canton Bulldogs which went 9-0-1 in the year. At that point the team moved into George Halas' Decatur Staleys and was 10-1-2 by the end of the 1920. The team moved from Chicago to Chicago in 1921. They took home the AFPA title with an overall record of 9-1-1. Chamberlain's fame was born during the championship game against Buffalo after Chamberlain took a capture back 90 yards to score the game-winning score. He jumped into his team the Canton Bulldogs in 1922 and the team took the title with a record of 10-0-2 and a shutout of nine of 12 opponents and allowing just 15 focus points during 12 games. The team was led by him in scoring scoring seven timeswhich included two when he was able to capture the return of a catch attempt.

Returning in Canton for 1923. In 1923, the player won one more championship as the Bulldogs finished 11-0-1 and eight shutouts, and a consolidated from 246 focuses and 19 wins against.

Canton was moved to Cleveland during the 1924 season, but Chamberlain was still the most successful player, leading his team to a record 7-1 to win a record-breaking third title. He was an instructor and player in The Frankford Yellow Jackets out of Philadelphia during the following two seasons but injuries cost him a couple of games. In 1926, the Yellow Jackets went 14-1-2, beating out 10 NFL competitors. Chamberlain continued his playing profession until the age of 33. He played in the Chicago Cardinals in 1927 while also serving as a coach. A statue of Chamberlain is located in Southern Elementary School in Blue Springs, Nebraska.

Facts and figures

1. It was reported that the Muncie Flyers played in only one game during the inaugural season of APFA and disbanded in the after being dismantled with a score of 45-0, by The Rock Island Independents.

2.

2. 3 record. They were tied with Cleveland 7-7. They finished the season with consecutive tie-breakers with Buffalo as well as Decatur.

3. It was the Green Bay Packers' first season in the APFA was in 1921 when they won 3-1. The club remains there in Green Bay ever since.

4. The Chicago Bears took their new form in the 1922 season This means that they typically outdo Green Bay by one year in terms of the longest-running team of the NFL.

5. In 1922, there existed groups from each of the four currently NFC North urban areas-the four urban areas of Chicago, Green Bay, Minneapolis and Detroit.

6. Red Grange finished only 24 passes in his career but 10 of those scored touchdowns.

7. Red Grange had two of the coolest nicknames in NFL history: the Galloping Ghost as well as The Wheaton Iceman.

8. With a record of 58-16-7 Guy Chamberlain has the best winning percentage (.759) among any coach in NFL history , with at minimum 50 wins.

9. Guy Chamberlain stays the main mentor throughout NFL history to win championships with three different teams.

10. The affiliation was quite uncomfortable in 1925, when Dayton (0-7-1), Columbus (0-9-0), Duluth (0-3-0), Milwaukee (0-6-0) as well as Rochester (0-6-1) were merged to make a total of 31-2.

11. Paddy Driscoll scored in excess of 65 focus times during his professional career and also a career high of 86 spots in 1926.

12. Paddy Driscoll 55-yard field objective record, which was set in 1924, lasted 29 years before it was it was broken with Bert Rechichar in 1953. This record stood for 17 years before it fell to New Orleans' Tom Dempsey who hit the record with a 63-yarder in the year 1970.

13. The Green Bay Packers turned into the leading group during NFL history to claim three straight championships consecutively in 1929-31.

14. The Packers were 34-5-2 during the zone, a record performance of 85.4 percent.

15. 1934 was the year that the New York Giants turned into the main group, with a variety of mistakes to take the association title after they finished 8-5 to be victorious in the East Division,

then, after that, smashed with the 13-0 Chicago Bears 30-13 in the championship game.

Trivia Questions

1. What was the total number of groups that participated in the initial period that comprised the APFA?

A. 10

B. 12

C. 14

Chapter 2: The Rapid Expansion (1930s-1950s)

What the Great Depression may have done to the NFL. It actually reduced it to ten groups at the start in 1931's season. However, instead of becoming an unimportant footnote, the league joined together and put franchises in areas that would support their needs. The number of franchises dropped to eight in 1932, but the idea for a new concept emerged from the division of the league in two sections, each one of which was able to create an hero who would play in a championship game at year's close. The announcement of the draft was made in the midst, as did the primary game was broadcast on public television. There was a resurgence of bigotry during this time however, in the 1950s the sport had become its school in the same way as its popularity.

Playoff Fever

The New York Stock Exchange declined on the 29th of October 1929, which triggered the start of the Great Depression that endured over 10 years until it was over when the United States walked out on to join the Allied reasons in World War II.

There were twelve teams within the NFL in 1929, but the number of teams dropped to 11 of every 1930 , and 10 in 1931. The Boston Braves were involved in the conflict in 1932. However, Frankford and Providence were eliminated, as was Cleveland and Cleveland, leaving the league with just eight teams: Boston, Brooklyn and two teams from Chicago, Green Bay, New York, Portsmouth, and Staten Island.

The 1932 season was over with the question of which team should compete for the title of association champion. There were three teams: the Chicago Bears were 6-1-6, the Green Bay Packers 10-3-1, and the Portsmouth Spartans were 6-1-4. The Packers were the team with the highest winning percentage, but tie-ups were removed from the standings, meaning that Chicago as well as Portsmouth were both as 6-1, with Green Bay was at 10-3. The Packers were omitted in regards to the final game of the season and resulted in the 9-0 Bears victory for the title.

The owners met before the start of the season, and decided to split the organization into divisions. Each division was a participant in a championship game, which left it to be decided who the top group in the organization was. The association was split in two divisions, the East division as well as divisions of the West division in the season of 1933. The East comprised in the New York Giants, Brooklyn Dodgers, Washington Redskins, Philadelphia Eagles, and Pittsburgh Pirates The West comprised of it's Chicago Bears, Portsmouth Spartans, Green Bay Packers, Cincinnati Reds,

The Chicago Bears and Chicago Cardinals. There was no question this time around as the Giants won their place in the East with six wins and an 11-3 record and the Bears by 3-3 games , with an overall record of 10-2-1. They fought with each other in their NFL Championship game the Sunday before Christmas, with Bears getting a 23-21 victory in front of a crowd of 26,000 spectators at Wrigley Field.

Bill Karr scored the second of his two final scores with a 19-yard parallel to bring his Bears back to victory. In a battle of styles and styles, the Bears surge (49 transmits to 161 yards) defeated the Giants with their pass play (14-of-20 with the 208-yard score). This was also a victory for the 30-year-old Red Grange, who was in his second year of the NFL. The following season, both teams faced off again in the title game, with the Bears playing in the championship game 13-0, outscoring opponents 286-86. Meanwhile, the Giants had a record of 8-5 with just 11 focus per game, and relying on a flexible safeguard. Both teams had played one month earlier, with the Bears having a slam-dunk victory in a laugher of 27-7 as the Giants made six mistakes. The second game, which was played in front of over 35,000 spectators and a record crowd, saw the Giants present one of the more spectacular gatherings ever in NFL history. After 3-3 at 3/4 the game, they exploded for 27 positions in the final quarter. Ken Strong scrambled for scores of 11 and 42 yards. He also kicked two focus. Ike Frankian snared the ball for 28 yards by Ed Danowski, and Danowski scored after an eight-yard run. Each of Chicago's three quarterbacks had a catch and the Giants defeated the Bears with their renowned surging game with just 89 yards on 46 conveys, which is a standard for 1.93 yards per attempt. In the meantime the Giants scored 173 yards on 37 conveys, and pounded out Strong's 94 yards in just nine attempts. This was the final NFL game played at the Chicago's Red Grange.

Bronko Nagurski

It's hard to imagine anyone with a favorite football nickname in place of Bronislau"Bronko" Nagurski. His family was foreigners from Ukraine as well as he played an all-American guarded fullback and tackle for three consecutive seasons in the University of Minnesota from 1927-1929. He was part of the fascinating class to be inducted as a member of the Collegiate Hall of Fame and the Pro Football Hall of Fame during the two traditions the first time they had long period of time. In the United States, he was a migrant from Canada and later became an expert in lumber during his teens, and was able to define the massive, sturdy casing. The most memorable game he played was at the 1928 season at school in which he reclaimed an injury while the Badgers were preparing to win the match, and jumped to six

consecutive times for a score. At the point of scoring the defense blocked the give guard to secure the victory.

Three seasons in his time with the Gophers, they finished 18-4-2, and they won a Big Ten title game in 1927. At 6 feet, 2 inches and 245 kg, Nagurski was greater than many linemen in the NFL and wore an 18-inch ring, which was the largest at any time in the NFL as well as an 8-inch head protector. The year 1932 was when Nagurski made the game-winning score pass towards Red Grange as the Bears defeated in the final against the Portsmouth Spartans to win the NFL title. In the next year, he took home another title with Chicago. While the details were not included in the scores during his first two years, Nagurski was a hit regularly, starting each of his 13 games as the newest kid in the league in 1930, and scoring five points. He was a tractor on a regular basis with a tally of less than 4.8 miles per conveyance but scoring scores, with seven in the Bears in 1934's undefeated regular season.

In the middle of the football season Nagurski became an expert wrestler who was in addition, a well-known actor. He was awarded five titles in wrestling during his time and was honored by the Wrestling Hall of Fame in 2011. He quit Bears in 1937. Bears in 1937 at the age of 29, only to be able to come back into the team in what is believed to be told as a straight-from-the-page story the pages of comic books, or some folklore.

In 1943, six years following the last time he played, he came back with the Bears and, as with every NFL team were missing a number of their former players because of the US contributions to World War II. He was in the team for eight games, but also displayed the skill of averaging 5.3 yards of convey. The Bears were 8-1-1 in winning their division, and beat in the title game against the Washington Redskins 41-21 in the NFL championship game. Nagurski transferring the ball several times for 34 yards before scoring the game-winning touchdown.

World War II and the NFL

Football's bravery isn't as great as the courage of soldiers. When the US declared war on Japan and then Germany at the end of the 1940s, players and certain mentors were either drafted or added to the roster by the dozens. When they Brooklyn Dodgers opened instructional course in late spring 1942, only seven their players were remaining. There was a vacancy in the Cleveland Rams suspended play for the season of 1943, and they Pittsburgh Steelers and Philadelphia Eagles united forces to become the Steagles and split home games between the two communities in

1943. In 1944, the Steelers along with the Chicago Cardinals converged in 1944 and then the Boston Yanks converged with Brooklyn during the season of 1945. A total of 21 players from the NFL were killed in combat during World War II, 19 of them former or active players, along with an ex-lead trainer and an organization chief. Three military personnel-three of them - Maurice Britt, Joe Foss and Jack Lummus were awarded the Congressional Medal of Honor, the most prestigious military award within the United States. Britt was a player in the Detroit Lions in 1941, later he was sent to the war as an assistant lieutenant in Arkansas following the season. He was the detachment's chief during the infiltration into Sicily during 1943. In the course of Operation Shingle, he did exercises on the display of enemy lines in order to discover the location of a hidden Nazi automated rifle house. He was awarded the Distinguished Service Cross for this display of chivalry, and was the primary beneficiary of the top four battle adornments awarded to an infantryman during World War II. He was later promoted to lieutenant in the chief of the legislature of his native territory of Arkansas.

Foss is a Marine pilot who was a pilot who provided 26 warriors against foes throughout his time in the Second World War He was then appointed as the Governor of South Dakota and filled in as the chief of the AFL between 1960 and 1966.

Jack Lummus played school at Baylor University and was an outstanding football and baseball player. He was a player with the New York Giants on the turf in 1941. After the team's championship game that year and he joined the Marine Corps saves. In the following three years, he was part of the first troop influx to land in Iwo Jima. 14 days after the assault following the liberation of three fortresses of the enemy and an explosive landmine and lost two legs during the blast. Even with medical treatment and an 18-inch blood bonding pints and a bucket of blood, he threw the bucket that was on the table for surgery. His doctor kept in touch with his mom "Jack suffered very little because he was not able to live for long. I met Jack just a few minutes after being hit.

With a calm, smooth and smugness Jack declared, "The New York Giants lost a decent man. All of us lost an honest person."

In a field of dynamic players, the star of the battle was Giants offensive tackle Al Blozis, who chipped despite being aware that he could be a home-based player since his height--6 feet 6 inches, 250 pounds--wasn't within the limits of the draft. Blozis was a top shot-putter in Georgetown and also set the US Army record of the longest throw. In the month and a half later to his participation in the NFL championship match, the player was shot dead by German machine guns while searching for a lost watch within the mountain ranges of France.

A final note: Though he may not have been known to the NFL at large for long, there was also a 19-year old University of Texas green bean who

The group joined was a part of the Army Air Corps to stay in the air. He was stationed at London and flew 30 missions in all and survived an accident landing in Belgium. His name? Tom Landry.

"The Rams Go West

The Cleveland Browns started out in the AFL in 1936 prior to transitioning to the NFL from 1937 to 1945. They were mostly terrible in the initial years, going from 1-0 to every year, with their only non-losing record of 1937-1944 being in 1939, when they were 5-5-1. As World War II slowing down and the war fading away, the Rams appeared to be out of the blue growing in 1945. Pat Waterfield showed up to be a quarterback after his four-year stint in the University of California at UCLA as well as being named NFL MVP during his debut season after being selected into the Fifth Round. Waterfield led the team in offense , racking up 1,627 yards similar to scores passes (14) and yards per game (9.4). On Thanksgiving Day He wiped out on the Detroit Lions for 339 yards. The game also saw Jim Benton become the main player in NFL history to achieve 300 yards in a game. He scored 303 yards on 10 occasions. The record was held until 1985.

After years of being mats after years of mats, the Rams beat of the Bears (17-0 and also 41-21) and beat the Giants in the open (20-7) and then defeated of the Packers (27-14 in 20-7). Their most notable mishap was 28-14 at Philadelphia. The victory over the Lions brought them the division title and they then played some of the more exciting championship games in the history of the league beating Washington 15-14. Waterfield played two score in front of crowds of 32,000. Waterfield was married by Hollywood entertainment star Jane Russell. One month after the name, Rams' proprietor Dan Reeves amazed fans and counterparts when he announced that the team would move into Los Angeles, the primary NFL team that is west of the Mississippi River.

Reeves was forced to relocate the team since buying it in 1941. The group was not prepared for the upcoming Cleveland Browns of the All-America Football Conference according to the previous Ohio State mentor Paul Brown advised the team. The move was a snare to Cleveland however it had a huge impact. One of the facets of the condition of the organization that was leasing at the Los Angeles Memorial Coliseum was the assurance of using African-American players. It was tough to resist the lure of keeping working in LA. The population had increased from 319,198 from 1910, to 1.5 million in 1940. In 1950, an additional 380,000 had been added until 1960, when the number of people living in the area was 2.479 million.

The team went 6-4-1 the first season, but fell to .500 until 1949, when they were 8-2-2 and won the West but losing in the title game to Philadelphia Eagles in the title game, which was 14-0. The year 1950 saw two seasons-ending games were played during the season, as the Browns and Giants were tied with the Giants for East title, and the Rams along with The Bears to win the West. The Rams beat Chicago 24-14, however Cleveland was the only city to suffer. Cleveland was punished when they withdrawal from the Rams. The Browns were victorious in a 30-28 thrilling trip on the night of Christmas, and reviving from a deficit of 28-20 with 10 unanswered points in the closing quarter. It was the Browns' Otto Graham was an all-star team that destroyed the opposition with 22-of-33 passes, racking up 4 scores and 298 yards and rushing for additional 99 yards on 12 conveys. 1951 saw another quarterback from Los Angeles, as Norm Van Brocklin won and led the Rams had a tough divisional title, which took them to the title of public champions with an 8-4 record. They were behind 7-4-1 Detroit and 7-4-1 San

Francisco as well as 7-5 Chicago. Waterfield as well as Van Brocklin consolidated to toss for 391 yards, and 26 touchdowns. The Rams faced the Browns again to claim the title. They won the title thanks to the score of 73 yards from Van Brocklin to Tom Fears.

A look at the Ugly Face of Racism

Black players made a splash at the start of APFA as well as the NFL with nine players getting ready. The achievements that was the Carlisle Indian School football crew which included the legendary Jim Thorpe, opened the possibilities of the association for others Native Americans. In the Dayton Triangles, Dayton Triangles utilized Asian-Americans Walter Achiu and Arthur Matsu, and Hispanic players Ignacio Molinet and Jess Rodriguez were members in 1927. In the following season, every dark player was exiled of the organization without any explanation and none of them was ever a part of the NFL between 1928 and the year 32. One of those two players was Fritz Pollard, who, together with Bobby Marshall, were the first two African American players in the NFL. Pollard was the most prominent black player of Brown University in the

US, which was where he studied Chemistry and was a starting halfback when Brown took home its first Rose Bowl. Two players of color, Joe Lillard and Ray Kemp were members of the league in 1933. However, Lillard was kicked out of by the Cardinals because of his fighting style for the ball, and Kemp was left alone to search for a job after training. He was a player for his team, the Akron Pros, who won the AFPA Championship in 1921, and was also the mentor for Hammond Pros. Hammond Pros in 1923-1924.

The major part of the strategy to stop dark players from joining the NFL was developed in the hands of Washington Redskins proprietor George Preston Marshall. The NFL banned dark players from playing in the NFL until 1946 which was when they were drafted by the Los Angeles Rams were

Reintegrated in the agreement for lease of the Los Angeles Coliseum, their new home. The Rams identified Kenny Washington and Woody Strode in 1949. By that time various groups began using draft singles to exclude African-Americans. However, not Marshall however who stated that he would start employing"coloreds after they were recruited by the Harlem Globetrotters began recruiting whites." In the year 1962 Marshall came up against his rival in the role of US Attorney General Robert F. Kennedy. The Redskins 30 year lease on D.C. Arena was due to expire. The arena was controlled by Washington D.C. government. Kennedy stated that unless Marshall had a dark player as a recruit and the government would refused to pay his rent. Marshall finally resigned and picked Syracuse All-American defensive back Ernie Davis as his #1 selection. Davis was aware of the situation and requested an exchange which resulted in the Redskins receiving an African-American All-Pro Bobby Mitchell, who developed into an Hall of Fame wide receiver.

The All-America Football Conference

The NFL was born after World War II, and suddenly, football that was proficient was the topic of conversation for every finance manager in the United States. Although the NFL had a specific number of facilities however, the number of athletes who were able to graduate from high school was staggering and it was enough to Chicago Tribune sports editorial manager Arch

Ward, who established the organization in June 1944. He enlisted a variety of wealthy financial backers who had failed to establish institutions of their own. Ward had previously urged the NFL to grow, but was disqualified. However, he presented his idea of the All-America Football Conference (AAFC) with teams in Buffalo, Chicago, Cleveland, Los Angeles, New York as well as San Francisco. Miami and Brooklyn were added later. The organization was planning to launch in 1945, but held for one year following the conclusion the war. World War II. The organization was founded just one time after Cleveland had lost its city. Cleveland dropped it's Rams at Los Angeles in the wake of winning a championship.

Then came the Browns and their coach Paul Brown, who had been the winner of six titles in secondary schools throughout Ohio in the state of Ohio at Massillon High School and the 1962 title for the public in Ohio State. The NFL was affected by the new league especially Redskins owner George Marshall, who saw his coach and a number of players leave for the new Baltimore adoption beginning in 1946.The AAFC was well known from the beginning. Curve was able to use the press to get amounts of publicity, the association was the host of forty of the College All-Stars, and air travel was now in use, allowing the association to establish teams on the ground in Florida as well as California. The first game of the association took place on the 6th of September 1946. A crowd of 60,000 were present to see the Browns beat in the Miami Seahawks 44-0. This was the largest ace football team in the history of football. The team was generally successful and Cleveland defeated its rivals the New York Yankees 14-9 for the first title. NFL popularity also increased and both associations were in a fierce battle for players, and sending their compensations that were soaring. For each of the big teams, only two made a profit in the ace game in 1946-The Browns along with the Bears.

The most memorable season for AAFC was 1947. The 49ers secured freedoms of the Army's Mr. Inside Felix Blanchard, and Mr. Outside, Glenn Davis. A match of the New York Yankees and Los Angeles Dons attracted over 82,000 people in Los Angeles, and The Browns beat the Yankees to win the title. The title was reclaimed in the next year, with the 9-0 Browns beat the 10-0 49ers in front of 83,000 people in Cleveland. The Browns took home their third consecutive championship and the outcome was undisputed: the association was extremely uncomfortable. The team collapsed in 1947, which reduced to seven the AAFC by seven. Cleveland took home a fourth straight title, and was able to improve to 52-4-3 unrivalled. In the late 1950s the two organizations merged. In late 1949, the Browns, 49ers, and Colts joined the NFL and the Dons were joined by the Rams. After a couple of months the event it was the time that it was the World Series of Pro Football was played against the NFL championship Eagles as well as the AAFC champion Browns. In the eyes of 71,000 people who were gathered in Philadelphia on the day it was the Browns won a crushing 36-10 victory. The next year the Browns defeated their rivals the Rams during the NFL title game to claim their fifth straight title.

Sammy Baugh

The glory of Temple, Texas, Sammy Baugh was among the greatest quarterbacks of NFL history. He took home two titles and was named to the group of the primary, All-Pro multiple times, and led the team in passing yards multiple times, and also in scoring scoring elapsed scores twice. He was also an outstanding punter, and astonishingly led the club in careful catch-ups, with 11 out in 1943. His average rate of 51.4 yards per kick in the year 1940 is however the NFL record for today. It is ironic that he really needed to be a star player and signed a grant with Washington State University, just to injure his knee while as it slipped into a respectable midway point just a month before his departure for school. The grant was later revoked.

He chose TCU considering everything and was an en two-cross AllAmerican and was named MVP of the very initial Cotton Bowl. The spring before his junior year George Marshall offered Baugh $4,000 to play for the Redskins. All the time, he was trying to get a chance to play.

He was ace at baseball and didn't sign the deal until the day of an All-Star Game, where the collegians defeated their opponents, the Green Bay Packers 6-0. He was the 6th selection in 1937's NFL draft and ended up with a score of $8,000. In his first year on the block he led the Redskins to an NFL title, setting an industry standard for the fulfillment of an entire season that saw 91. In the game against the Bears He was only 17-of33 for 335 yards. He also scores passes of 78, 55, along with 33 yards in the victory of 28-21.

Baugh was not called up during World War II and took the Redskins to an second title at the seCond in 1942 defeating Bears Bears 14-6. He completed a score pass and then threw an 85-yard dropkick. The year 1943 was when Baugh was regarded as having the most impressive individual season of his career in NFL history, leading the league in drop-kicking, passing and blocking attempts. In 1947 on Sammy Baugh Day in Washington D.C. Baugh tossed at 355 yards, and six points. In the midst of retiring in the year 1952, he set 13 NFL records. He then became a mentor for players from the American Football League's New York Titans and Houston Oilers. He passed away in 2008, the only remaining member of the first Hall of Fame class.

Sid Luckman

Sid Luckman was the best Wing-T quarterback of all time, an NFL MVP and the holder of the four Chicago Bears NFL titles somewhere between the years 1939-1950. He was first recruited by the Steelers but was later traded for the Bears. Luckman is required to be convinced by Halas to take up football, believing he'd be employed by his father's shipping business. The moment Halas arrived at Luckman's house and signed a contract to pay $5,000, things quickly changed. The following campaign, Luckman drove the title game against the Washington Redskins. They Skins have won the initial match 7-3, but over the next few weeks, Luckman, Halas, and the obnoxious planner Clark Shaughnessy had added a "man moving" issue to the T-developmentprocess, one that the Redskins were unable to fix. The Bears ran the ball several times, gaining 381 yards, while keeping the Redskins to just five yards in 15 attempts. The Redskins were able to turn the ball to the north nine times during 73-0 in a mishap, which was the highest unbalanced score of all time in NFL history.

Following the conclusion in the season of 1943 Luckman was a part-time Ensign in The US Merchant Marines. He was granted permission to join the Bears when he was stationed in the US, but was unable to practice with the team. In spite of that, he played for the team with a passing tempo in both 1945 and 1946 despite having only started 7 of 21 matches he participated in. He drove the team in score for both years. In 1943 He drove the group in yards (2,194) and score passes.

(28). His average that is 8.4 yards per effort is second only in the history of Otto Graham. He led the team to additional championships during 1941, 1943 and 1946. He also owns the record for two Chicago Bear passing records in spite of the fact that his career ended in 1950.

Chuck Bednarik

Chuck Bednarik was perhaps the most offensive scream to ever time, and he was a skilled footballer. As the top selection in the 49th NFL draft The player played every single one of the 13 years with the Philadelphia Eagles, was an eight-time Pro Bowler and a ten-time first group All Pro and double cross NFL champion. Before he ever reached the NFL however he joined the Air Force and flew 30 combat missions in Nazi Germany, being granted the Air Medal, four Oak Leaf bunches as well as the European-African Middle East Campaign Medal, as well as the four Battle

Stars. From there it was his turn to Penn as three-time All-American at linebacker, focus and punter. He was a focus in 1969 and given a vote for the greatest focus of all time. He was the final fully-time athlete of NFL history. In a game that was played under severe weather conditions in 1949 the Eagles defeated their opponents the Los Angeles Rams 14-0 for the NFL title, completing an 11-1 record for Philadelphia.

Bednarik was just 35 years old age at the time the Eagles took home their second title however, his season of 1960 is most likely to be his best acknowledged. He was 6'3 and weighing 233 pounds, the man was a true giant of the game. In the year 1960, in an Eagles-Giants match, he was able to even out Giants running back and awardee Frank Gifford, an eight-time Pro Bowler, and the league's the MVP of 1956. It took Gifford 18 months to recover from the injury, and he was forced to quit the NFL the following year. Gifford returned the following year and played for three additional seasons, but never as an offensive back. After a couple of months the incident during the NFL championship game in the title game, the Eagles were able to drive Green Bay

17-13. Running back of the Packer Jim Taylor got free, however, Bednarik had him pulled.

in the open field near the 8-yard mark down in the open field at the 8-yard line, and laid over him as the final couple of minutes were ticking off the timer to announce the title.

Night Train Lane Train Lane

Richard "Night Train" Lane was the exemplification of the bigoted attitude Redskins owner George Marshall dreaded with regards to AfricanAmerican players joining the NFL. Lane wasn't just great but he was also unfathomable. After four years of service serving in the Army He was employed at an aircraft factory situated in Los Angeles, lifting

Metal sheets that weigh a lot. He rode his vehicle regularly to work, and he rode by the offices that were part of The Los Angeles Rams. He kept a book of clasps from the secondary school as well as junior school and had to be given his shot as an open collector, but was shifted to guard back. At his first scrimmage the head coach Joe Stydahar said, "Path was here to build his mark on the team. Actually, just the night before, the player

59

was offered a job." He was initially averse to the name he chose for his nickname of Night Train and thought it was might be too bigoted, but it was actually derived from a recording of Jimmy Forrest that he preferred to move to. He gave it a higher level a chance at pleasing when a newspaper listed what might be the greatest game title each time Lane destroyed Redskins player Choo Justice. The paper was headlined with"Night Train Devails Choo." Then, in the year 1952, his first year as a player, Lane played twelve games and attempted 14 block attempts, which is an at present standing NFL record. He scored two return scores, one of which was a 78-yarder and also drove the team by capturing 298 yards in attempts. Then, in January of 1954, he made the switch for The Chicago Cardinals and again drove the club by grabbing picks, but this time with 10. From then on the teams ceased to throw towards him on the other side of field which made him a lot more prone to injury. He was traded again with the Lions 1960. In their first win in the period He snatched an Johnny Unitas pass and returned the ball 80 yards to score the touchdown.

Facts and figures

1. In their thrilling victory during the 1934 NFL championship game The New York Giants scored more than a focus in the last period (27) more than they did in 12 of their earlier games.

2. Sammy Baugh's 335-yard pass in the NFL championship game in 1937 stood as the postseason record for tenderfoots until 2012.

3. Baugh was selected by the MLB's St. Louis Cardinals, but was let go when he didn't have enough time to play as a Double A.

4. In the 1943 victory in the battle against Detroit, Sammy Baugh tossed four scoring passes on offense and was involved in four interceptions on defense.

5. In 1945, Sammy Baugh finished 70.33% of his runs (128 from 182) which was a record that continued to be broken until the record was broken Ken Anderson (70.55) in 1982.

6. Chuck Bednarik missed just three games over his 14 seasons.

7. The Chuck Bednarik award is presented each year to the most cautious footballer in the school.

8. Night Train Lane as well as Don Doll, the player who was traded to him, are the two main individuals in NFL history to have more than one time period of interceptions that were 10+.

9. Lane was unable to block an additional point, and was able to block a 42-yard block that was returned for a score during 1962's Pro Bowl. The following day , he was able to have his addendum taken away. 10. Lane's terrifying tackle by face mask Jon Arnett prompted the association to change its rules the following year, and preventing taking control of the mask.

11. In 1944 In 1944, in 1944, the Brooklyn Dodgers changed their group name to the Tigers.

12. The Boston Yanks failed in 1949.

13. The most prominent aspect that was this was Baltimore Colts collapsed after its debut season as a member of the NFC (1950).

14. The Dallas Texans were conceived out from the cinders that made up the New York Yanks, just to merge after a single season.

15. The Baltimore Colts joined the association in 1953.

Trivia Questions

1. Who won the NFL final game, the 1933 title match? A. Chicago Bears

B. New York Giants

C. Philadelphia Eagles

D. Pittsburgh Pirates

2. Who did Sammy Baugh break his record for 335 yards of passing through a tenderfoot during an end-of-season game?

A. Dan Marino B. Peyton Manning C. Russell Wilson D. Matt Ryan

3. Who was the group that George Halas persuade to draft and trade Sid Luckman?

A. Rams B. Steelers C. Browns D. Giants

4. How many times during his 14 years of service was it that Night Train Lane not have an interfering incident during the entire season?

A. Zero B. Zero B. C. Three D. Three

5. Which were the most popular groups in the NFL towards the end of 1959?

A. 10

B. 14

C. 12

D. 16

Answers

1. A

2. C

3. B

4. B

5. C

Chapter 3: What Is American Football?

The answer could be the the first lesson we are taught in this journey. You might be wondering, what made me decide that I added 'American' after football? That's a good question! The second reason is that there are two reasons I chose this route. The first is that 'football' as it's referred to in different parts of the world, specifically Europe, is the soccer we play in! It's true, in the event that you go to Germany and start muttering "football that" and "football this," the great folks of Germany are likely to think that you're speaking about soccer. To clarify, there exist another two famous soccer leagues around the world that are not soccer: The Canadian Football League (CFL) and the Australian Football League (AFL). Both leagues have different rules from our own league, the National Football League (NFL) and could provide an excellent subject for a subsequent or even a third book. Important to keep in mind: This book is focused on the NFL!

(Courtesy from unsplash.com.)

Now that we've got that out of way, let's begin to understand the details of what this chapter will be about. However, it is not possible to dive straight into the action without knowing a more about the fundamentals. In this section, we'll discover a bit more about the history of football as well as how the sport has evolved through the years. The changes focus on issues like uniforms, league changes, and safety for players.

It is important to understand the fundamentals of the game to be able to comprehend the various terms and definitions as we increase our knowledge about this wonderful sport!

What and when Football Was Developed?

If you consider all the bizarre rules or regulations that are part of a typical football match, it begins to ask "Who invented all this?" For this, we must look back to the 12th of November in 1892, which was more than 100 years ago! It was the day on when players from the Allegheny Athletic Association football team defeated Pittsburgh Athletic Club. Pittsburgh Athletic Club. While none of it was particularly important and football was played prior to this, but it marked the very first occasion that that a footballer, William 'Pudge' Heffelfinger, was paid to play in the game. The player was compensated $500. a sum that is more than $15,000 today in terms of modern standards. It's not bad for a single game you know, Mr. Pudge!

Much to the delight of few, football began by combining two sports both soccer and rugby into one fun game. The first football match ever played was played between Rutgers in 1869 and Princeton on the 18th of May, 1869. It was not until the 1880s however the rule changes made in the 1880s took the game as a wild one and turned into the game we are familiar with and cherish. The man who conceived the rule changes is Walter Camp, a rugby player from Yale.

"By the 1880s, most athletic clubs had a football team" (ProFootballHallofFame, n.d.). Unsurprisingly, college players greatly enjoyed the game's competitive element and the games were extremely intense and often broke out into fights! As a contact sport it was a method for students to let off their anger after a tiring day of school.

All of this helped create the conditions for the famous Allegheny Athletic Association vs. Pittsburgh Athletic Club showdown (AAA against. PAC). Both teams were seeking an edge on the competition in what quickly turned into a heated rivalry. It was PAC However, it was the PAC which eventually offered Pudge to join their team which legally made Pudge the first professional athlete ever.

Following the match both teams continued to look around the region for players with better skills to improve their chances of beating opponent when the next opportunity arose. The PAC went to Chicago and returned quickly to Pennsylvania for a second matchup against the AAA. In this game the PAC decided to pay Pudge and Knowlton "Snakes'" Ames who are part of the Chicago team to represent the PAC in the upcoming match with the AAA.

The AAA however, was not taking the decision at face value. "Thus aware to the situation, the AAA did some scouting on its own and discovered that Ben "Sport" Donnelly who is a star player as well as Ed Malley would play with the AAA ..." (n.d.).

So, both PAC and AAA were armed with a bit of "extra ammunition" to play in their next game.

The game ended with only one score scored by Pudge that resulted in a score of 4-0. If this sounds like a strange scoring to you, it's congratulations! In 1892, touchdowns could only be scored four points and not as many points as they do now. If you get an score (cross the ball over the end zone of the opponent) then you're allowed to kick an additional points (field goal) worth one point, or "go for two" that is, place yourself near the opponent's goal line , and attempt to score a second time to earn an additional two points. Note: Two-point convert: If this doesn't succeed then you don't get the single point you would have received in field goals. In this case there is a bit of risk/reward taking place!

The classic game between AAA and PAC produced the AAA making a net income of $621 for AAA and PAC, which is more than $16,000 today! While the game was slow and not very high-scoring but it did show that even in the beginning there was plenty of cash to be made in football, for the players and owners!

Who was the first to invent it?

In contrast to the basketball games and baseball, for which there is a single source of inspiration, the history of American football is somewhat complicated. While some claim to trace the beginning of the sport to the 1820s, other assert that the sport was not made legal prior to the "Pioneer Period" between 1869 and 1875.

Many historians and football fans are of the opinion with the idea that Pioneer Period bred the true roots of American football we have today and cherish it to this day.

As I mentioned earlier the first football match that is known to have taken place was played between Rutgers University and Princeton University on the 6th of November 1869. The game took place on Rutgers field, with two teams with 25 players each who tried to score by throwing the ball over their opponents' field goal. Throwing or carrying the ball was not permitted! Rutgers took the win by a score of 4-4. This was not quite as thrilling as the 42-39 matches we're used to watching in modern times However, the game was definitely exciting for the spectators.

The game was nevertheless physically brutal and resulted in more than a few gallons of blood lost.

The game sparked an "football trend" across the nation as more and teams adopting the game as it increased in popularity. In 1873, nearly all universities in the United States were playing football in some form playing before a crowd of spectators.

This was the first step in the path to Walter Camp, widely regarded as the "Father of American Football" (Wikipedia, n.d.). Camp as a player and a rules visionary was the one who first suggested in 1880 to decrease the amount of football players on each side of the field from 15 (it had been reduced between 25 and 15 just a couple of years earlier) and increase it to 11. Although the proposal was not accepted initially, the modification was eventually adopted in late 1880s. Today eleven is what Walter Camp proposed 141 years ago (and still counting)!

Camp's most well-known change However, it was a rule that has endured the test of time. "...the introduction of the line of scrimmage, and the snaps from center to the quarterback also adopted in 1880." I'll to break down these four terms in a short time, since they can all be confusing to those who are unfamiliar with the game.

Line of Scrimmage the area where the ball begins in the possession of a team's. After the kick-off, this will be where the ball will be set up for the team to attempt to move through the field and score. When a team finishes an pass or plays the ball forward (or in reverse!) it moves to into the area where the line of scrimmage is to be used for the following game.

Snap The snap isn't the type of Thanos snap! The snap is the movement that the ball is passed an quarterback's hand by the central. It begins most plays. Each player will be able to move beyond into the line of play prior to it is time to snap the ball.

Center This is the center player that throws the ball towards the quarterback. They are the center one of five linemen. Offensive linemen are regarded as one of the most powerful players in football. they are responsible for protecting the quarterback.

Quarterback: When you think of about football, you're probably thinking about the quarterback. Tom Brady, Aaron Rodgers, Peyton Manning, Joe Montana Joe Namath, Aaron Rodgers -- all quarterbacks! A quarterback will be the person who takes the signal at the middle and determines (with the defenders running at him!) what he's planning to do with the ball. The ball could be handed an running back an athlete designed to it, run up the field. Or you can run it yourself or give the ball over to his teammates.

We'll learn much more about each of these terms in the near future and I hope this helps make the statement somewhat easier to comprehend.

In retrospect the way we see it, our friend Walter Camp wasn't done revolutionizing the game. Although his initial plan was to establish the rules of scrimmage to boost the activity of players and increase the excitement of the game However, he soon realized the teams, Princeton, in particular utilized the new techniques of their players to keep hold of the ball for long time periods, and to draw players out. That is, his strategy was a failure! In 1882, he then introduced the rule of distance and down which required teams to travel at the minimum of five yards over three minutes or to hand over the ball to the opposing team. The rule was later expanded and is used today in the modern day of American football, in the form of four games for at minimum 10 yards.

Other rules introduced by Camp included the ability to tackle players below the waist as well as the use of referees and scoring regulations and halves. These rules, to a certain extent, continue to be used in today's game.

(Courtesy from unsplash.com.)

Camp was a retired football player in 1882, but he remained as a participant at rule-based meetings until his death in 1925. "The Walter Camp Football Foundation continues to pick All-American teams named in his memory" (n.d.).

A true pioneer in the game, Walter Camp and his numerous rule changes establish the basis for the modern football is played to this day. Walter Camp is the most important pioneer of American Football and is considered as one of the most influential people in the history of football (despite being only the span of a few months).

However, while his rules was considered revolutionary in the time, the rules would continue to alter over the years as football became more advanced. In the next section we'll explore the way rules have changed since the 19th century, and how they change to this day.

How Football has changed over the years?

As with people, sports change and change over time. While certain rules from old football were appropriate for the time but rules change constantly to meet the demands of safety officials, fans and players.

The NFL now has an Competition Committee to change rules and modify the game as they think it's appropriate.

Although rule changes are made fairly quickly to enhance the safety of players, this wasn't the scenario in 1920, when the NFL was established in 1920.

When the rules were to be altered it could take years or even decades to get that change to be implemented. Rules can now be altered every year!

One of the first major changes made by the NFL occurred as a result of the first NFL playoff game played in 1932. The match was conducted between Chicago Bears and the Portsmouth Spartans. "In the match, Chicago Bears fullback and future Hall of Hall of Famer Bronko Nagurski was caught in a fake plunge then backed off, leapt into the air, and then lobbed a throw towards Red Grange for a key score in his team's 9-1 triumph" (NFL, n.d.).

In the game players (or whoever was in possession of the ball) was not permitted to throw the ball from anyplace beyond 5 yards from the line of scrimmage. This means that the ball-handler must be at least 5 yards back from the line where scrimmage was throw the ball. In 1933, to the outrage Portsmouth demonstrated following this incident, the league altered the rules so that players can throw the ball any point within the line of play. This rule remains in effect today.

Since the beginning the NFL has said that it alters rules with the sole purpose of making the sport more enjoyable and enjoyable for its players. Hugh "Shorty" Ray an inductee into the NFL's Hall of Fame thanks to his alteration in the way the sport is played "...crunched the figures and found an immediate correlation between higher attendance and more scoring" (n.d.). This led to the league with rules that would increase the entertainment value of the game, which fans welcomed with enthusiasm.

Over the next 30 or so years the league began to cool on the new changes, and then went into a stagnation as teams began to focus on running football more instead of passing the football. This resulted in fewer games, less thrilling play and a lot of frustrated fans.

In 1974 the NFL introduced a new set of rules to bring back excitement into the sport. The new rules included:

Removing the goalposts 10 yards makes the kicks more difficult.

All field goals missed over the 20-yard line will result in a quick turnover, meaning that the opposing team will receive the ball the point where the kick was missed.

Kickoffs are moved away from 40 yards to 35 yards which results in more high-contact play.

Eliminating penalties for offensive plays.

The rules listed above along with a few others were designed to add more excitement and intense action to the game.

What's the result? A spike in passing yards per game and dip in running yards per game. While running the football is an essential aspect of football that teams continue to play in modern-day football however, the league has concentrated on being an active pass-based league which has been which is much to the joy of its fans! A 30-yard passing field is much more thrilling than a 5 yard run.

The current rules were designed to make the game more excitement. Just a bit later down the timeline, NFL imposed restrictions regarding"chop blocks," which is "chop block" which is a very dangerous technique where two offensive players run across the field, and then block a defensive player one high and one at a low level, resulting in numerous knee injuries for defensive players. The chop block in the current NFL is a 15-yard offense, so the team that has took the offense must return 15 yards prior to the next game!

Whatever your opinion regarding what you think of the NFL as a sport however, it's amazing to watch the NFL experiment and try new rules. It's something other leagues such as those of (Major League Baseball (MLB), National Basketball Association (NBA) and National Hockey League (NHL) often struggle with.

What are the Uniforms have changed and why

When football was first introduced in the latter part of nineteenth century, there was barely any uniforms to be found. There were no helmets for players or shirts that were ragged, and were padded only in the smallest of places. As the sport has grown it's uniforms have changed. With the advanced technology available and better equipped to detect head injuries, and also to design extremely elaborate helmets that help keep players safe.

The Helmet

The first time helmets was worn during a football match was during the 1893 match in the 1893 game between Army as well as Navy. There was a growing awareness among players to notice the risk that playing football could be for neck and head injuries, and so some players considered bringing helmets into the mix. However, it wasn't until 1939 but helmets were made mandatory for teams of football across the nation.

"The first helmets worn in football were constructed of mole skins that were bonded to safeguard players who had an interest in their own safety" (Daughters 2013). These basic designs failed to protect players from injury and so they were relegated to "ear flaps/aviator models" later on.

The 1930s as well as the the 40s In the 1930s and 40s, the first helmet made of plastic was introduced through Illinois trainer Robert Zuppke. Although the helmet was not without several initial disadvantages, such as price and demand they eventually prevailed and took the leather helmets of the past out of business.

In the following years players and teams started to decorate their helmets to show off their school pride. The helmets were typically colorful and featured cool logos and mascots for added design points!

Beyond that but the bright helmets may help quarterbacks to see their receivers in the field. Receivers are those who move across the field in order in order to find an opening to pass. Because of their colorful helmets the quarterback will be able to discern the colors of his team against. the colors of the opposition.

In the 1970s, Riddell established the standard time by introducing the HA range of headgear with vinyl pads within the helmet which were filled with air in order to take the impact away and provide an improved fitting (2013).

Riddell is now the most renowned helmet maker and collaborates closely with researchers to ensure that the safety of players and their comfort are protected by their helmets.

Although safety is the most important thing making sure that the helmets are at the very least comfortable is an additional feature to have!

The Facemask

It's much more difficult to pinpoint the source that led to the use of facemasks. Since football was played by college students who wanted to release some sweat, it's not a surprise that punches and jabs were thrown at players' faces throughout the game. It led to players putting on nose guards and other devices that resembled medieval ones to protect their faces.

In 1953, it wasn't until when Riddell created a special facemask for Cleveland Browns' quarterback Otto Graham. It wasn't the first football facemask however, determining the exact first facemask is a nearly impossible feat!

(Courtesy from unsplash.com.)

For Graham his facemask, it was constructed using the Lucite shield. Although it looked smart on paper, the Lucite was prone to the habit of breaking on the impact, an issue that later led to it being out of the NFL.

This resulted in Riddell using an BT-5 helmet that had an integrated single-bar facemask and thereby opening the floodgates which would eventually lead to triple-bar, double-bar and all sorts of customized masks you find in the NFL in the present.

Like their helmets Riddell collaborates with scientists to design the safest facemasks for maximum security.

The Shoulder Pads

Strangely enough, the concept that protecting your upper body when playing football is way before the idea of safeguarding the head. The idea of shoulder pads was conceived by L.P. Smock in 1877. Smock was an Princeton college student in the year 1877. These first shoulder pads were constructed from wool and leather and sewn into jerseys.

It was only in late in the 1970s, and the 1960s that the shoulder pad were able to catch with helmets of the day. Moving between leather and plastic made these pads to grow slimmer and stronger for greater durability.

When the materials change, so too did the places shoulders pads are used to protect. At first, they were used to cover only shoulder joints, pads began to extend into the body and protect areas like the ribs and upper chest.

The visual change in shoulder pads from the early 20th century might appear to be among the shocking changes to the equipment. What began as a simple method of protecting shoulders of players turned into a functional cocoon.

The excellent padding also enabled players to appear stylish and fast contrasted to the bulky pads of the 1990s. While it may not seem to be important to us elegant padding and looking stylish on the field are vital to players because they have many eyes watching their appearance.

The enhancements made to the new pads can be "...more than skin-deep because the improvements result in better ventilation, increased mobility, improved comfort, and greater safety" (2013).

The Pants

As compared to the helmets and shoulder pads they haven't been altered considerably since the game's beginning around the turn of the century. The football pants with padding were introduced to the game before the facemask and helmet, as they were worn by the majority of players from the end of the 1880s.

Similar to the shoulder pads, early football pants were made of canvas with pads stitched into the pants. Then, evolution made to its highest point until hip pads were also added.

Similar to the other gear we've been discussing up to now The gear has become thinner, more elegant, and more comfortable for the modern day player.

Concentrating on nylon as well as various synthetic fabrics, the purpose for the trousers is to make them very comfortable, yet invisible.

The Shoes

They are also known as cleats today. It's amazing that the first college footballers could move like they did with boots like devices that they were wearing! They were heavy, slow and awkward.

Strangely enough, it was not the emergence of technology that led to the creation of upgraded footwear for players, similar to other pieces of equipment we've seen. Instead it was created, partly, by people who wanted more competitive football. The best athletic shoes will mean more traction and greater games taking place on the football field.

Another aspect that influenced this choice was that players were required to plan for any weather conditions. While the boots performed well during a sunny day it was likely to become more difficult when it started snowing or raining. These factors together helped to create the cleats.

Learning from the pros in players in baseball as well as European soccer. Cleats were introduced with the addition of metal to their footwear to give themselves more grip during the cold winter.

In the end, designers removed the boot's design completely and went for the more modern, sleeker cleats.

The Ball

Football isn't possible without...well...the football! It's no shock to anybody who understands everything about the game that ball, as well as American football are very similar in the same way. The ball for rugby is similar in shape, however slightly bigger and constructed of various substances.

It wasn't always this way however. The ball that was first used in the first game played of Rutgers as well as Princeton in 1869 was the sour mix of the ball of a rugby team and the soft basketball. The ball was unable to hold its shape and was difficult to throw, kick and even to hold!

The first leather football was invented in 1887, and was developed by Spalding who were than the other companies of the time for the creation of footballs rather than baseballs. Although the ball was ungainly and blunt to both ends, it appeared closer to the modern football of as of today than the ball utilized in the Rutgers game against. Princeton game.

"Over time, the pointed ends of the football increased in prominence and made the body was streamlined due to the simple process of evolution and necessity rather than a dictated rule" (2013). Also, as with the rest that football has, it's the way the ball changed.

A fascinating, less-known fact regarding the ball's design is prior to 1956, teams played with white footballs to play at night, making it more visible in darkness. Although it was later changed to brown footballs featuring white stripes there's an additional interesting aspect that goes from this notion: Though the NFL ended up removing the white stripes on its football, the college football didn't. Even to this day colleges utilize a brown ball that has white stripes whereas their NFL ball remains brown.

The 32 NFL Teams

Then, we can get into the fascinating story of the past. In the current NFL landscape the league has 32 clubs that stretch across the whole country all the way beginning from Los Angeles to New York City. In the next section, I'll look at the 32 teams, explain the way they came to their famed name, and when the team initially formed.

1921: Green Bay Packers

The Green Bay Packers, the first NFL team was named for their first sponsor which was that of the Indian Packing Company. These weren't movers. "Packers" was a reference to meatpacking, which was a job that was very popular in the area in the early days.

The Green Bay Packers are widely regarded as to be one of the best teams in NFL history The Green Bay Packers won the first two Super Bowls ever with legendary head coach Vince Lombardi.

The year 1922. Chicago Bears

Then, a year after one year later, the Chicago Bears were formed. If you look at the Chicago Bears' name, it is important to keep in mind that at the time baseball was a lot more popular within the United States than football. Therefore, the Bears chose the name Bears due to the fact that it was closely connected to another Chicago team that was called the Cubs.

In choosing the name as a the same vein as an MLB team The owner tried to woo Cubs' fans Cubs and turn them into Bears supporters.

Another note to note is that Bears was chosen for the team's name since the owner believed that NFL fans, in general are bigger than baseball players.

1925: New York Giants

It took three more years for yet another group to be added to the battle. It was an organization that was from in the Big Apple. Similar to that of Chicago Bears, the New York Giants attempted to take names from the MLB team, and also. They succeeded, adopting the name of the Giants name from MLB and incorporating it as their official name.

Beyond that More than this, the Giants also symbolized the numerous tall buildings that are located across New York City. The name seemed appropriate on both sides.

1925: Arizona Cardinals

It would take a long time to allow the present Arizona Cardinals to make it to Arizona The team was founded in 1920. However, they didn't make it in St. Louis, at the time, until. The name was

derived from their uniform color ...a cardinal red.
It was not related to birds!

1933: Philadelphia Eagles

The football world considers them as one of the
most enthusiastic and active fans, the
Philadelphia Eagles fans love their Eagles and love
their city and love the color green and white!
Eagles games are typically noisy, loud and lively,
even though they're not always child-friendly!

There was a long absence of nearly 10 years
before another team was added to the team the
Philadelphia Eagles were another team named for
a bird, despite not related to the bird. The name
was chosen to pay tribute to the president
Franklin D. Roosevelt's National Recovery Act of
1933. Although they eventually became
competitive however, the Eagles faced a lot of
difficulties in the years following their founding.

1933 Washington Redskins

The now defunct Redskins currently called The
Washington Football Team due to the racist
background of the mascot. It was created
because their owner wanted to be connected to

people of the Native American people around the region. However he also wanted to distinguish his team from his rivals, the Boston Braves. So his name Washington Redskins was settled on. Washington is the only team that has lost its original logo due to racism.

1934: Detroit Lions

A less tense history of the origins is that the Detroit Lions wanted to be similar with their MLB team that is that of the Detroit Tigers. Additionally, they were determined to be the ultimate ruler of the league, just like the lion who is the king in the wild.

In a twist of irony, Detroit is among the very few clubs in NFL history not to win an award.

Although their aim was to establish a monarchy but that is one that they're striving towards!

1937: Los Angeles Rams

In the following three years the group was added. It was the Rams. Perhaps the most boring story of origin of all the NFL teams, the team's owner Buzz Wetzel chose the name Rams since his most favored football team in college was Fordham Rams. It's simple, in essence, that he took the name of the school!

1940: Pittsburgh Steelers

In 1940 in 1940, the Pittsburgh team had the brilliant idea of letting Pittsburgh residents choose the team's name. In the first ever successful name-that-team contest, an idea that was later taken over by other teams -- it was one steelworker from Pittsburgh who came up with their name Steelers. With the rough and tough character in the town, Steelers name was a hit!

1945: Cleveland Browns

Another team which may not have an element of originality when it came to choosing their name. The Cleveland Browns were named the Browns in honor of the General Manager/Coach Paul Brown. For a quick reference General Managers are the team's supervisor and is responsible for issues like trading of players, coaching, as well as the drafting of players. The coach is the one who runs the team in games, making plays, communicating with his players, and employing strategies to ensure that his team wins. Paul

Brown played both of these roles for the Cleveland football team and so they paid tribute to him by naming the Browns. The team's mascot is not a human however, it is the dog!

1950: San Francisco 49ers

It's unlikely to require an engineer to solve it! Since the 1849 gold rush occurred in part in California It was appropriate to that San Francisco football team to pay tribute to that by calling themselves the 49ers. Another interesting factis that the 49ers have the distinction of being the sole team within the NFL that has an identifying number as component of its name.

1953. Indianapolis Colts

Although the Colts have moved around like no other group it appears they've finally settled in Indianapolis after a few visits to Baltimore (who later adopted as the Ravens). The Colts were named the Colts due to the fact that Indianapolis is well-known for its horse breeding, particularly close near the arena. This, along with the natural selection of a mascot to be something frightening like a horse, created the Colt an obvious and well-liked choice.

1960: Dallas Cowboys

Although they are the team of America however, they are not the most popular team in America. Dallas Cowboys came onto the scene quite late. The Cowboys picked this name due to their desire for a slice from Texas culture. What speaks of Texas more than the image of a cowboy riding a horse to battle? There are very few things!

1960: Denver Broncos

Another team that benefitted from a team name competition included one of the teams that won was Denver Broncos. The Broncos were named for many reasons. one, the founders of the football team were enamored of the Bronco due to its characteristics like grace and toughness in the playing field. Additionally than that, the Denver region has always been known for having wild broncos that live within the region. This is a great match!

1960: Los Angeles Chargers

In 1960 the NFL was a huge success! One of the teams this year was the Los Angeles Chargers, a team that was initially based within San Diego.

Another team benefiting from a name-that-team contest, Chargers was the team's name. Chargers was selected early due to the fact that the manager at the time loved the idea of the team's name resembling the "Charge!" chant which was heard at numerous sports occasions. Today the battle cry is still heard during Chargers game.

1960: Buffalo Bills

Another team that is named after an individual named the Buffalo Bills honored Buffalo Bill Cody the legendary American soldier who hunted buffalo and showman. With only one professional club in the town--the often-maligned Buffalo Sabres of the NHL--the Buffalo Bills have one of the largest supporters of the NFL.

1960 New England Patriots

Another team, another name-that's-team contest, this time with the New England Patriots. The Patriots are thanks to Tom Brady (we will learn more about the legendary quarterback in the future) The Patriots are closely tied together with their fellow team the Steelers as the team with most wins during NFL the history of football (6). The name was picked to honor and honor to the soldiers from their country United States bearing the same name during the Revolutionary War.

1960 Las Vegas Raiders

Another tournament. The name was chosen as raiders have been known to be excellent combatants. Similar to the Bills they are also good fighters. Raiders may not have championships over their lengthy history, but they possess one of the largest fans in the league. They often dress up as full Raiders in black and silver face paint. Moving far more frequently than the other teams of the NFL, Oakland still loves their Raiders even though they currently live within Las Vegas.

1961: Minnesota Vikings

Burt Rose, the general manager of the Vikings picked the name due to the fact that Vikings were proud people with a desire to be successful. In the past it was the case that Minnesota Vikings were the only team in America. Minnesota Vikings had the distinction of being the first team in the country to represent the whole state (Minnesota) as opposed to just a particular city.

1963 New York Jets

MetLife Stadium which is stadium that is home to the New York Jets, is one of the best arenas of the NFL because it is home to not just one, but two NFL teams! Certain Sundays it's an home for the New York Jets. On other Sundays, it's an home for the New York Giants! NFL schedules must ensure that they don't duplicate shift between the Jets and Giants otherwise one of them could be left without a venue for Sunday games!

Of all the teams that play in the NFL and the NFL, the Jets might be the most intriguing in acquiring their name. In the beginning, they were planning to change their name to the New York Dodgers. However, the Los Angeles Dodgers, one of the most legendary clubs within MLB history, resisted the name and refused to permit this to happen. They tried a variety of names but none stuck. Then, they chose the Jets due to the simple fact they knew that Shea Stadium in New York at the time was situated close the LaGuardia Airport. From all the motives to choose a name, this is probably the most straightforward, but it is also the most authentic!

1963 Kansas City Chiefs

It's not the most politically correct choice today however the reason why the Chiefs picked their name in 1963 was due to the fact that many of Native Americans lived in the Kansas City area. Already seeing teams such as those of the Washington Redskins and Cleveland Indians being forced to change their names and teams such as those of the Atlanta Braves (baseball) and Kansas City Chiefs may be forced to change their names in the near future.

1996: Atlanta Falcons

In the context of Atlanta The Falcons first appeared on the scene in the year 1966. The name-that-team contest was also a part of the game and the Falcons being chosen due to the fact that they are a formidable and notable hunter. Beautiful bird and distinctive mascot selection The Falcons are among my top mascots of every league.

1966 Miami Dolphins

Another cool and distinctive emblem The Dolphins were selected for Miami because of the animal as being among one of the "smartest and fastest creature of the ocean." While the "smartest part of that description is probably accurate, it's important to consider that they're not the fastest animals on the sea. For instance, killer whales and barracuda, swordfish and sailfish all move more quickly than dolphins. But that, the mascot of the dolphin was an excellent choice!

1967: New Orleans Saints

Like the Chargers moniker, New Orleans Saints were based on the well-known "When The Saints Are Marching In" song. It was loved by the people from New Orleans during the Mardi Gras celebration, it was an obvious option to honor the song's classic melody by choosing the name that was associated with the song.

1968: Cincinnati Bengals

The answer is simple It's simple: It is simple: Cincinnati Bengals of 1968 were named after an earlier Bengals organization from the same city, which lasted from 1937 until 1941.

1976: Tampa Bay Buccaneers

The Bucs have named themselves after pirates of the 17th century who attacked on the Florida coast. The name is among the most well-known names in the NFL as is the enormous pirate ship that shoots real cannons following every Buccaneers score at their stadium home. If you're in Tampa and you want to go to the Bucs game, be sure you stay away from the ship...it's was known to trigger some scary jumps!

1977: Seattle Seahawks

It is believed that the Seattle Seahawks' nickname was selected due to the fact that the birds are plentiful throughout The Pacific Northwest. The seahawk is famous for its ferocity. This is evident to the supporters too. They're among the most loud, intense, and active fan bases in the league.

1995: Jacksonville Jaguars

One of the most recent clubs in the NFL The Jacksonville Jaguars got their name due to the fact that a zoo in the state contained the name of a Jaguar. The most fascinating aspect of the tale is the design of the Jaguars helmet. It is remarkably similar to the logo that Jaguar utilizes for its luxurious cars, the automobile company threatened to sue Jacksonville Jaguars if the team didn't modify their logo. They Jacksonville Jaguars obliged, avoiding an ugly confrontation that could have been a disaster for a large corporate.

1995 Carolina Panthers

The Panthers sought to distinguish themselves from their opponents by opting for light blue colors and the mascot to be elegant, stylish and strong. They haven't yet won the title however, they've appeared at two Super Bowls within the beginning 26 seasons. This may not sound like much but it's not an awful beginning!

The year 1996 was Baltimore Ravens

Perhaps my most preferred reason for choosing a name is that it is that the Baltimore football team chose the Ravens in honor of Edgar Allen Poe's famous poem with the same name. If you think this is a bit bizarre, it will make more sense when you consider that Poe was one of the Baltimore native. Beautiful, sleek and dangerous Ravens from Baltimore are to be as unpredictable and dangerous like Poe himself!

1999 Tennessee Titans

The Tennessee club was looking to pick an appropriate name for their team, one that demonstrated the strength, courage, toughness and perseverance. So, the Titans were formed. The coaches and owners have adopted the name as their own and have also taken it to heart. Over the seasons the Titans have displayed a consistent desire to run the ball tough and hit their opponents with more force! They're the definition of a tough team.

2002 Houston Texans

The only team to be established during the 20th century the Houston Texans chose this name due to a focus group that gave the team three options: The Apollos, the Stallions along with the Texans. These are all excellent choices, but it was the Texans name was chosen in the end.

Chapter 4: Fundamentals Of Football

Once you've acquired a little more about the past of the game as well as the NFL along with the 32 clubs that comprise the league, it's now time to get into the basics that govern the sport.

Football is a far more intricate sport than many think. Although it appears like a simple process: see the ball, take it, but there's a variety of positions that perform different tasks at the football field. with coaches making decisions about which plays to call, and referees who make sure that the game runs smoothly.

Within this section, we'll discover the basic principles of football and the way it plays; rival leagues trying to (and have attempted) to take on the NFL and also the various positions on the field of football along with the rules and moves across the field.

The basics of football

If you've never seen football before even the most basic aspects can seem difficult to comprehend when watching the game in full-speed. By breaking down every element my aim is to teach you the fundamentals of football, without overloading anyone!

Basics

The aim for the sport, more than everything anything else, is to get the ball across on the field (by either running or throwing it) toward and eventually to the opponent's goal zone. The zone of the end is a 10-by 53-yard area of the field where defensive players attempt to protect.

(Courtesy from unsplash.com.)

For a touchdown to be scored, which is crossing the ball into the goal zone, it has to be accomplished through either running with the ball over the line of goal (the entry point to the zone of finalization) or by throwing the ball to a player into the zone of end. The details of touchdowns can be difficult to comprehend--we'll go into more detail later on--but players must be able to take the ball from an opponent with their feet in the zone of end to count as an actual touchdown. The officials determine whether the player's feet were successful in catching a passing score.

Downs

Downs are perhaps the most important but also the most confusing component in this American soccer game. The offensive team is required to get the ball moving across the field during a play. The field measures 100 yards by 53 yards in width.

In any place where the team is starting by kicking the ball that is the first lines of scrimmage. We were introduced to this concept in the initial chapter and this line is the place where the ball will begin (horizontally) throughout the whole field. When the initial line of scrimmage has been counted the offense will have four plays to get it 10 feet across the field. This line is referred to as"the marker for the first play..

When they pass the marker for first down in less than 4 minutes the whole process is reset! The brand new line of scrimmage that is set and the first-down marker will be set 10 yards to the left of the field. The team, as always is given four plays to make it to this new mark.

Important note Note: If a first-down isn't gained from the offense during any play occurring on the first or second down, it doesn't suggest that they should return to their initial lines of play! Every time a team gains yards that line shifts upwards to meet the spot where the game ended. When the game is longer than the marker for the first down, the play is moved to the second down , and so on.

When the team that is on offense is unable to get past the first-down marker in just four games, the possession is switched to the opposing team. Naturally the team that holds the ball will typically attempt to kick an attempt at a field goal, or even punt it before doing this. Field goals are worth 3 points . It is the time when an offensive team's kicker is on the pitch and kicks into the uprights. Punts occur when a team is aware that they won't make it to the first down marker and wants to pass the ball to another team. Through punting, the offensive team may make the opposing team's initial field position more difficult as opposed to if they try to get it on the fourth down, but fail.

Although the majority of scoring happens near the end zone, touchdowns could be scored at any point within the field. That is the player doesn't need to stop running after you reach the first-down marker. The goal is to get a touchdown! The score of a touchdown can be worth six points, and field goals are equivalent to 3 points.

Plays

Plays are the intricate activities that take place on the field at any particular down. When I was younger they were straightforward and involved an athlete running the ball forward for just a couple of yards. Since then the game has evolved evolving, changed, and transformed into a passing-focused game. That means that there are now more tricks and more sophisticated plays and more methods to move the ball along the field quickly during any game.

The plays are typically directed by the head coach or the offensive coordinator or even the quarterback. We've already discussed the quarterback and head coach and that's the role of the offensive coordinator. one who is specifically appointed to assist in the design of the offense for the team.

While most plays are closely linked to offensive players, it is important to remember that defense players must also call plays! They are typically called by the players who are on the field the head coaches, or even the defensive coordinators.

The offensive team has 40 seconds to either put the ball on the field or kick the field goal. In the event that an offensive player is not able to catch the ball during this time, they are punished with a penalty that takes the ball five yards backward. The game clock is constantly reset. game clock which will reset at 40 seconds after every game.

Timing

Contrary to soccer that is played in half, American football can be played in four quarters , with 15 minutes per quarter. When there's an incomplete passing, the clock ceases. The clock can also stop when a player goes beyond the bounds of his territory with less than two minutes left in the second third or fourth quarter.

Each team receives three timeouts in each half. Timeouts may be used by anyone in the field, but generally, they are commanded by the the head coach. They last for 30 seconds , and permit the athletes to have a short break.

The halftime show lasts for 12 minutes typically, however, it can be prolonged to 20, 30, or even more in championship games (for instance for the Super Bowl). It is believed that the Super Bowl halftime show involves an appearance by a popular artist and is viewed as more like a party as opposed to a halftime show that is about football!

Additionally the 10 minute extra time period in case both teams remain tied after conclusion of the 4th quarter. If the playoffs are in progress the duration is extended up to fifteen minutes.

In overtime, both teams will flip a coin in order to determine who will get the ball in first. The team with the ball has one full opportunity to move across the fields and achieve the goal. If they) fail to score,) make the field goal or) give the ball to the defense team, the team that began as the defense team takes over.

If the team who starts with the ball, it turns into the defensive team, who is able to score a touchdown during the same game then the game is over. If the first team to receive the ball fails to score a touchdown , but does manage to score an attempt to score a field goal, the defensive team has the chance to equalize that score and win by scoring the help of a score. After the initial game, each team will play alternate possessions until one team wins regardless of score.

Scoring

As stated the value of touchdowns is 6 points, while field goals earn 3 points. A touchdown is scored by putting the ball in the goal zone of the opposing team. In American football the scoring play is examined by referees in order to ensure it's legally scored. This includes checking to see whether the ball crossed the goal zone, or if a player had both feet on the zone of end with possession of the ball. If all of these factors are satisfied the touchdown is considered a success!

The three other methods players can earn points is listed below:

Extra point Extra point executed by the kicker after an errand and is worth, you guess it, one point.

Two-point conversion: Rather than making the extra point in the wake of scoring, teams could opt to score two points. The two-point conversion is a single-play that begins at the two-yard line of the opponent. If the team wins two points, they will earn 2 points. If they fail to score and they are stopped, they will receive zero. They cannot score an extra point following an unsuccessful two-point conversion. An interesting note is that if the defense gets an unintentional fumble by the team that is going for two points, they are able to return it to the middle of the field, and then score 2 points for themselves. This is among the most uncommon plays of football, however it can happen.

Another way to earn points is through a safety. Safety occurs when a player is able to put the ball in the end zone of their team and is then tackled against the defensive team. The defense team is awarded two points and gets the ball returned following the next kickoff. This is a game that isn't seen often, yet it's always thrilling when it does.

Positions

The positions of the football team are difficult to comprehend and even more difficult to learn. I will try my best to clarify each of the areas to the greatest of my abilities. Let's first take a an examination of the offense.

Quarterback A quarterback will be the one who takes the ball from the center. He may occasionally play calls to his squad. He is the one who throws the ball down the field, and is the most important player on an whole football team. The quarterback is equipped with an audio headset that is built into his helmet that allows him to talk to his offensive coordinator and coach during the game.

(Courtesy from unsplash.com.)

Running Back(s) The running backs (full and half) are among the toughest jobs on the football pitch. The most important player on offense the full back gets the hand-offs from the quarterback and tries to get to the field without being attacked. Half-backs are another possibility for plays that require running. In today's NFL running backs are expected to assist in blocking and catching passesas well. Running backs are among the often injured positions in football due to of the abuse they endure from opponents.

Wide Receiver(s) The number of wide receivers is typically one to three players in the field at the same time. Wide receivers take routes to open up so that the quarterback can pass passes to them. These receivers are generally the tallest and fastest athletes on the field, which helps enhance their catch radius.

Tight End(s) Tight ends are a different position that is becoming more and more sought-after in the current NFL. Tight ends used to be utilized to assist offensive linemen (we will discuss them shortly) block quarterbacks and running backs and not much else. As the game has grown and the tight ends have become more versatile, they are now used more as wide receivers. Another position that receives much punishment from defenders, tight ends must be quick, strong and tough to withstand some of the punishments they receive.

Tackles Two tackles on an offensive line a line that was created to shield the quarterback from being harmed by the defense. On each offensive line, there's a left tackle as well as a right one. The tackles are positioned on the most distant parts of an offensive line (the two outside spots on the opposite side) and are usually required to stop opposing teams' most powerful and fastest players. Offensive linemen have to block their offensive players (quarterbacks and wide receivers, running backs tight-ends) and seldom touch the ball by themselves. This isn't the most glamorous job, but it's essential to have a strong offensive line in order for every football club to win.

Guards: Located in mid-section of the offensive line The guards are located on the insides of the right and left tackles, and vice versa. Like the tackles there's a left along with a right-hand guard in each football team. Guards are typically asked to play a bit more running than tackles because teams tend to prefer running across the middle, instead of running towards the outside.

Center We finally have the center. If quarterback is the primary position for an offense and defense, then the center will likely be to be the second. The center is expected to perform a lot! He must talk to the quarterback in order to be successful in snapping. The center also needs to take on the role of blocking the nose tackle in defense, which is usually the biggest and toughest player that any defense can provide. The center must also snap the ball swiftly and be ready to block while making the space for the running back as well as guarding his quarterback. It's a tough position that requires the right combination of strength and intelligence!

For the defensive players:

Safety: Each team has two safeties . They represent the pair of players who are farthest away from quarterbacks and are therefore typically used to defend against passes. But the defensive coordinator could use the safeties to protect against the run too. Safeties serve as the final line of defense and when an offensive player is behind them, it indicates that the ball carrier is headed straight to the finish line!

Cornerback(s) The cornerbacks task is straightforward (in the sense of theory!). They're responsible for playing against the wide receivers of the team in opposition. Anywhere a receiver goes, the cornerback is there to follow. When a quarterback attempts to pass a ball an individual receiver it's the cornerback's duty to disrupt the pass, attempt to take over (catch) it or even tackle the receiver when the ball is caught. They can also assist with running backs in the event that they penetrate their offensive line.

Linebacker(s) Linebackers: There typically three players on the field to help any defense that is defending. The linebackers make up in the middle of defensive line just after the runner is over their defensive line (who we'll discuss in a minute). Linebackers are sometimes referred to as "quarterbacks of defense" as they are the ones who announce or take the signals from coaches, and then tell the other players what the game is. One of the most difficult positions in football, linebackers must tackle receivers, running backs tight ends, receivers as well as quarterbacks. They are sometimes playing the position of a cornerback as well when a tight player attempts to catch a ball. Without strong linebackers, a defense is probably not that excellent!

Defensive Ends There are two of them on every football team: a right and left end. The primary function of the defensive end is to attempt to connect with the quarterback and cause him to make poor decisions. They are generally quick, strong and are able to hit hard! They also have the responsibility in running plays to keep the running backs in check and prevent them from allowing them to reach the outside, where there's usually lots of space to run.

Defensive Tackles: Last but not least we reach defensive tackles. They aren't identical to offensive tackles since they are located on the side of the line defensive (which is typically comprised of four players, not five). The ends are at the other side on the line tackles are situated in the middle. The defensive tackles are actually monsters! They are strong, big and frightening, and are tasked with taking down the offensive line to take down the quarterback or to get close to running backs who is behind the line of the scrimmage. They literally bowl balls that can swiftly take out any offensive player, when they're not stopped.

And finally, the special teams!

Kicker is the person who is tasked with kicking field goals as well as kickoffs. Kickoffs are the primary game sport and involves the player taking the ball down the field, permitting the opponent to return the kick to the field.

Punter The punter is the final position we'll discuss in this brief introduction to the various positions which are covered, is the person who throws the ball in the event that the team isn't keen to make use of their fourth-down option. The punter is trying to place the team that is returning the ball in a poor position on the field, which means they must travel several yards in order to get the ball.

Other Leagues competing with the NFL

Although the competition isn't anything more than thrilling, a number of leagues have attempted over the years to be competitive with the giant of the NFL. These could be different leagues from the United States, leagues from different countries, or something other than that there have definitely attempted to steal a portion of the viewers off the NFL. In this article we'll examine some of the leagues close to NFL in size.

The United States Football League (USFL from 1983 to 1986)

The USFL was able to have a good time in the 1980s, when they tried to be competitive with the NFL. In the past, President Donald Trump even got in on the fun by purchasing the long-lived New Jersey Generals. The USFL was able to acquire two previous NFL players to boost their competitiveness with the NFL however the league was eventually shut down in 1986.

XFL (1991-2001)

There was an attempt to revive the XFL up to 2020 however, the league dissolved before it even started partly because of COVID-19. The first XFL was established by WWE chief Vince McMahon and tried to beat the NFL by introducing a more rough approach to its sports. The league was "promoted as a sport with less rules and greater hits...the league had games with sexy cheerleaders and names on the backs of player jerseys" (Barrabi 2020).

The XFL was quite popular initially but then quickly lost favor among fans and eventually cost McMahon more than $70 million.

United Football League (UFL, 2009-2012)

The UFL employed players previously from the NFL to create four teams that specifically challenged the NFL's rules of playing during the autumn (the period when the NFL is set to begin). The league was destined to fail from the beginning due to the low level of competition and the fact that there were only two teams. The league ran for 3 seasons, which was a surprise before crashing in 2012.

Arena Football League (AFL, 1987-2008 (2010-2019)

The AFL is distinct from the other leagues in this area because it was able create a certain niche during its two periods. In addition it was able to sustain its impact through both its iterations. It was played entirely indoors, with smaller fields, narrower goalposts and other adjustments to encourage an action-packed, more rapid game The AFL was able to attract some major names and an impressive viewership during its two years of existence. The league was able bring in 19 franchises at the same time during its peak, but the league eventually dissolved in 2019 , with only six franchises remaining.

Alliance of American Football (AAF 2019, 2019)

The AAF is a sad tale as the league was lots of potential. Only surviving one season due to financial difficulties The league received positive early reviews, due to the quality of the performance on the field and the players. They managed to attract several famous names from college football as well as the NFL and this resulted in competitive play and high attendance. Unfortunately it was not intended to last but it ended up closing before the initial season had even ended.

Chapter 5: The Best 20 Franchises From Nfl

History

After we've got past the difficult aspects of learning about the game and also a more about the positions, we are now able to begin to tackle things that are more enjoyable things. In this chapter, we'll look at some of the most successful franchises in NFL history , and how dominant they have been. Once you've mastered the 32 teams as well as their history it's going to be fascinating to find out which have had the greatest success since the beginning of the league!

The top 26 teams with the Most Champions

26. Seattle Seahawks: 1 Super Bowl win

The Seattle Seahawks have one Super Bowl victory in its 45-year history of play. This might seem like an insignificant number but getting to this Super Bowl in the NFL is a challenge beyond belief.

Seattle won their first Super Bowl in 2013 when they defeated their rivals, the Denver Broncos.

Under the direction of rookie the quarterback Russell Wilson, the Seahawks defeated the Broncos and won the game by 43-8! The game was never a contest and the Seattle defense being the key to their victory.

2013. The Seattle Seahawks had an excellent secondary, which refers to the players who make up the final line of defense we talked about earlier. This includes cornerbacks as well as safeties. Seattle relied on their defense in the year they played they nicknamed them"the "Legion of Boom."

The Legion of Boom was dominant during this year's Super Bowl, forcing two Peyton Manning (quarterback for the Broncos) interceptions, as well as creating a safety too.

On the offensive side, Russell Wilson was effective with his throws, he scored two touchdowns and running back Marshawn Lynch scored an own touchdown.

Seattle has been consistently a great team ever since this Super Bowl win, but they haven't been able to win another since then.

25. Providence Steam Rollers: 1 NFL Title

For the keen-eyed viewers who are out there, you may be able to tell the difference in two teams: the Seattle Seahawks and the Providence Steam Rollers. Although the Seahawks have only one Super Bowl win, the Steam Rollers have one NFL Title. What is the difference between these two? Before 1967 in which the NFL officially joined with the American Football League (AFL) to create the current NFL The NFL was an independent entity. It was not until 1967 that there was a Super Bowl was born when the two major leagues merged to form one. The championships played in the NFL prior to 1967 are recognized as legitimate champions which is the reason one reason why Providence Steam Rollers have an NFL Title but not a Super Bowl.

This particular Providence Steam Rollers squad in 1928, the Providence team was so unique that they made it into the "NFL Top 100" teams ever, putting them at 98th. Even though they only played for seven years in the NFL and only seven seasons in the NFL, the Providence Steam Rollers will forever be remembered due to the incredible 1928 team.

As a team led with Gus Sonnenberg at running back The Steam Rollers went 8-1-2 (8 wins one loss, two tied) in 1928 and that was due in large part the defense which allowed 42 points during the entire season! This is amazing! In today's NFL teams are lucky to allow under 42 points over two games!

There wasn't a championship game prior to it was the Super Bowl, but the Steam Roller got their title by virtue of their winning percentage, just beating their second place Frankford Yellow Jackets.

24. New York Jets: 1 Super Bowl Win

The Jets are the only team to win a Super Bowl win in 1968 only one year after the merger of the NFL was established. It was a major transformation for the league as it was evident following the first two Super Bowls that AFL teams who joined the new league were not ready to match up against NFL powerful teams like the dominating Green Bay Packers. It was the Jets became the first ex- AFL team to take home this Super Bowl, handling the Baltimore Colts 16-7 in the 1968 Super Bowl.

It was led with "Broadway" Joe Namath at quarterback, who famously ensured the Jets winning before the big game The Jets finished the season of 1968 with an 11-3 record during their regular-season. The Jets beat their opponents, the Oakland Raiders in the semifinals and then beat the highly favored (and NFL mainstay) Baltimore Colts in the final.

Before the event, there was suggestions that the league might not be able to make it because the first NFL team was so powerful, and the AFL mergers were not! The Jets have helped to pave openings for league's transformation into the entertainment powerhouse it is now.

23. New Orleans Saints: 1 Super Bowl Win

The Saints made their way to winning a Super Bowl title back in 2009 when they managed to beat their opponents, the Indianapolis Colts by a score of 31-17. In a match against one of the most successful players in NFL the past, Peyton Manning, few believed that the Saints had a chance to win the game. With the help of their legendary quarterback, the now retired Drew Brees, the Saints were able to conquer the challenges and take home their very first Super Bowl title. Since since then, they've become a consistent team but haven't been able to get back to the Super Bowl.

This version of the Saints was a phenomenal offensive unit, ranked first in the NFL in terms of points per game. This was due in large part the play of quarterback Drew Brees as well as Wide receiver Marques Colston, who finished the season with more than 1000 receiving yards, and nine touchdowns. For wide receivers 1000 yards is an impressive goal to aim to when considering a great season. It's the same for running backs, even though their yards are from the ground, not. by air.

With a loyal crowd and an impressive team the New Orleans Saints squad of 2009 New Orleans Saints squad remains one of the best in recent times.

22. 1926 Frankford Yellow Jackets: 1 NFL Title

Another team that took home its title prior to the AFL-NFL merger in 1926, in 1926, the Frankford Yellow Jackets are considered to be a better group than the 1928 Providence Steam Rollers.

When the NFL published the league's Top 100 Teams of all time in the past few years in 1926, in 1926, the Frankford Yellow Jackets ranked 81st.

The team was based on the Frankford neighborhood in Philadelphia The Yellow Jackets were led by Hall of Fame Coach Guy Chamberlain who was also a player on the side. It is the Hall of Fame, I must mention is the highest honor each and every member of an NFL team strives to achieve. It is a prestigious club that is located within Canton, Ohio where only the best coaches, players owners, managers and owners are permitted to be honored there. If you're included in the Hall of Fame, chances are that you achieved something extraordinary during that football experience!

The Frankford Yellow Jackets were simply dominating, finishing second in the NFL for the number of points they scored per game, and second in the number of the number of points permitted per game. They finished 14-1-1-2 (14 wins, one loss, 2 tie) as the very first club that ever played in NFL history to score 14 wins in one season. It's an achievement that is still considered to be awe-inspiring in the modern world of.

21. Tampa Bay Buccaneers: 2 Super Bowl Wins

The latest team to be victorious in the Super Bowl, the Tampa Bay Buccaneers have already won two Super Bowls in only 45 years. That's not so bad considering how old it is!

The first championship for the Buccaneers was won in 2002. The 2002 Buccaneers team won it in the traditional way by leading in the field with their formidable defense, while also scoring sufficient offensively for them to take home number of games. The team finished 12-4 in the regular season before they defeated in the Super Bowl. Oakland Raiders in the Super Bowl with the score of 48-21. The Bucs in 2002 didn't have any pressure in the three games they played in playoffs. They began the playoffs by winning against their opponents the San Francisco 49ers by a score of 31-6. Then, they smashed the Eagles by a score of 27-10. Then, they smashed their opponents, the Raiders in the final game. The defense was fantastic and was led by three outstanding players, including the linebacker Derrick Brooks, defensive end Simeon Rice along with defensive tackle Warren Sapp. This was a team that scared the pants off of you.

The following Bucs team to be victorious in the Super Bowl came 18 years after the 20th century with the Tampa Bay Bucs defeating the Kansas City Chiefs by a huge margin of 31-9. The Bucs had a tough to make it through the playoffs having close matches against Washington Football Team (31-23), New Orleans Saints (30-20) as well as the Green Bay Packers (31-26) prior to winning over The Chiefs in the game of the century. It was led by Tom Brady, considered to be one of the greatest player in NFL history (more about him in the future!) The Bucs showed an amazing combination of defense and offense in their quest to win winning the Super Bowl title. On offense the Bucs had Tom Brady and wide receiver Mike Evans (1006 yards, 13 touchdowns) in the lead, while defense was extremely complete. With a team that is aesthetically pleasing in 2021 The Tampa Bay Bucs are looking for the third title.

20. Kansas City Chiefs: 2 Super Bowl Wins

(Courtesy from unsplash.com.)

The Kansas City Chiefs in the contemporary NFL are famous for several things: a high-powered offense, fantastic tailgating and a huge fan base! Participating in the two previous Super Bowls (and winning one) The Chiefs rank among the top teams on the NFL landscape.

Another team that has won the two Super Bowl titles are the Kansas City Chiefs. The first Super Bowl title was won in 1969, just as the combined league was in its beginnings. A formidable team that finished 11-3 in the regular season The Chiefs defeated teams like the Jets, Raiders, and Vikings to win their first Super Bowl. The Chiefs were led by a strong offense and a tough defense, the Chiefs were balanced and difficult to defeat on each side of the field.

In 2019, you'll find a totally more different model of the Chiefs. The team is led by the star quarterback Patrick Mahomes, the 2019 Chiefs are considered to be among the most impressive offensive teams of recent times. Mahomes was able to throw for more than 4,500 yards with only five interceptions in the regular season, and was more impressive during the playoffs. He was aided by the dazzling receiving tandem of wide receiver Tyreek Hill as well as tight end Travis Kelce, the Chiefs beat their opponents with spectacular plays, an abundance of scoring points as well as a dazzling offense. While they were able to enter in the Super Bowl the following season as the favorite however, they would ultimately be defeated by Tom Brady and the Buccaneers.

19. Miami Dolphins: 2 Super Bowl Wins

In 1972, the Miami Dolphins may be the most dominant squad in NFL history. They went 17-0 in a row (including playoffs) they Dolphins were the league's top team with the highest number of points scored, and were last in terms of points allowed. They simply took on opponents with ease and were led by the legendary Hall of Fame Coach Don Shula.

Offensively, they beat teams to the phenomenal running backs in Mercury Morris and Larry Csonka. Both ran over 1,000 yards of rushing this amazing season. The team did not pass very often and also dominated defensively by putting pressure on quarterbacks and stopping their runs. The only team ever to be undefeated and take home the Super Bowl, the 1972 Dolphins will be forever regarded as among the top teams to ever play.

It did not take Miami for long before they won another Super Bowl! Another Super Bowl came a year later in 1973. Although they weren't undefeated during the year (they suffered two losses) but they nevertheless plowed through the playoffs, and won the second consecutive Super Bowl trophy. The defense that was dominant stayed the same , while they changed their quarterback to Bob Griese, who threw 17 touchdowns. Morris Csonka and Morris Csonka were again the main players for the offense.

The Dolphins are a terrible 21st century team, to put the least, but are continuing to be a struggle this season.

18. Baltimore Ravens: 2 Super Bowl Wins

Although they've been around for two years in the Baltimore Ravens, the Baltimore Ravens have been a consistently excellent football team over the time span. In their coaching, they have taught things like dominating defensive play and running ball The Ravens can be tough frightening and formidable.

The first Super Bowl came in 2000 when they won 12-4. While they weren't exactly above average in terms of offensive performance however, this Ravens defense could be the best defense we've witnessed so far into the 20th century. They were strong, they were tough and they took on the offensive! The linebackers Ray Lewis and safety Rod Woodson the defense was able to strike terror into the eyes of any quarterback looking down at them. On the offensive the runners Jamal Lewis led the way with more than 1,300 yards of running in the season.

The following Super Bowl came in 2012 under the head coach John Harbaugh. A good team in their regular-season campaign (10-6 record) but the Ravens were able to get their gears moving in the playoffs, beating away powerhouses such as that of Denver Broncos, New England Patriots as well as the San Francisco 49ers (Super Bowl). The team was led by a great player Joe Flacco and star running back Ray Rice, the Ravens were able to rely on their defense to beat some of the amazing offensive teams they faced during the playoffs.

They are consistent and tough. The Ravens are nearly always playoff-ready and appear to be heading there again this season.

17. Arizona Cardinals: 2 NFL Titles

It's been a long time when it's been a while since the Arizona Cardinals have been competitive in the NFL. The team holds two NFL championships dating between 1925 and 1947. Although they've been around since the start that league was established in the year 1967 but the team has not been in a competitive situation and has only reached only one Super Bowl in the 2008 season.

The positive thing is for Arizona fans? The team of this year's Cardinals has the top records in the NFL. With a quarterback who is a rising star, Kyler Murray and a hard-hitting defense is this the year when the Cardinals get back to the top of the league?

16. Las Vegas Raiders: 3 Super Bowl Wins

The next step is to look at the teams that have won three championships. The Raiders were the dominant team during the latter part of the 1970s and into the early 1980s, winning championships in 1976, in 1980and 1983.

The 1977 Raiders began the celebration under the legendary Hall of Fame Coach John Madden. The 1977 Raiders won just one game, and defeated their opponents the Patriots, Steelers, and Vikings to claim their first championship.

In 1980 in 1980, the team was led by Tom Flores leading the team this time. The Raiders scored 11-5, and defeated them Philadelphia Eagles in the championship game with 27-10.

In the year 1983, there was time Tom Flores leading his team to a 12-4 record and the eventual Super Bowl title. A formidable offensive unit they relied on the star quarterback Marcus Allen and receiver Todd Christensen to help them get to the Super Bowl. After that, they swept Washington by 38-9, winning the third Super Bowl in just seven seasons. This was certainly an impressive period.

The Raiders have been able to field strong teams since then however they've not been able to recapture the glory and have been unable to return back to Super Bowl just once in the 21st century.

15. Los Angeles Rams: 2 NFL Championships as well as One Super Bowl Win

The first team to hold the distinction of having NFL title and Super Bowl and Super Bowls, the Rams are a legendary and proud team whether they play either in St. Louis or Los Angeles.

The NFL championships were won in the years 1945 and 1951.

After a period of good performance and good results, the Rams returned to the main game of the 1999 season in which they played their rivals, the Tennessee Titans. As their own St. Louis Rams, the team performed well on offense and defense placing in the top five positions in both of these categories. The team finished the season with a record of 13-3 The Rams were in a battle for the initial two stages of the playoffs having to contend with tough opponents like teams like the Minnesota Vikings and Tampa Bay Buccaneers. The difficult times didn't end there neither did the tough times continue. In the face of a fierce and determined Tennessee Titans team in the Super

Bowl, it was an intense contest between two teams that were very good. It was to the very last game and the Rams did their best to come through.

It was led by one of the most renowned quarterbacks ever, Kurt Warner, star running back Marshall Faulk, and great receiver Isaac Bruce, the Rams were an extremely difficult team to keep off the offensive.

The Rams continue to keep the tradition of a great offense going in their current form with a constant lot of points in the current NFL. They made it to the Super Bowl back in the season of 2018, but ended up losing against Tom Brady and the New England Patriots. They've been great this year.

14. Denver Broncos: 3 Super Bowl Victories

The experience of playing in Denver, Colorado, has many advantages. Apart from being one of the most beautiful natural settings of the United States with 300 days of sunshine and spectacular views of the mountains, Denver is also a mile up above the clouds (literally!). While that might not sound to be much to me or you the teams that are visiting must adjust to the high altitude and frequently have inhalers as well as extra air in the stands to help players who are who are struggling with the elevation.

Another proud team The Broncos have had three Super Bowl wins in the last 23 years...not an awful number at all! The Super Bowls were won during the 1997 season as well as the 1998 season and in the season of 2015.

In 1997 there took place during that year's John Elway show. He was the head of the Broncos had thrown for more than 3,500 yards and scored 27 touchdowns that season. Alongside legendary coach Mike Shanahan, the team had the most efficient defense in football. Elway was paired together with Hall of Fame running back Terrell Davis and Hall of Fame tight end Shannon Sharpe, was simply impossible to stop in both the 1997 and 1998 seasons.

It took Broncos fans another two years to claim another championship However, the eventual prize was in 2015, under Hall of Fame quarterback Peyton Manning in charge. Manning's season was not his greatest performance in terms of stats, since Manning was plagued by injuries and was struggling towards the conclusion the season. But Manning did enough offensively to allow his defense lead his Broncos into victory. The Broncos have been in decline since then, however, people in Denver are looking forward to a return to glory much sooner than later.

13. Canton Bulldogs: 3 NFL Titles

It's been a while since we've witnessed the Canton Bulldogs in action, however, they were a early giant of the NFL. The team won championships for the league during 1916, 1917 and 1919, this achievement stands among the top three dominating three-year periods during NFL history.

While the Bulldogs ended their existence 100 years ago, the history of Canton remains in the NFL. Its Hall of Fame, which I've mentioned before as an area where the top players and coaches as well as GMs are immortalized in the history of football and is located situated in Canton, Ohio.

12. Detroit Lions: 4 NFL Titles

While they've been among the teams with the lowest performance in the NFL following the merger but they Detroit Lions were a dominant NFL team in the past. They won championships in 1935 1953, 1952 and 1957 and 1957, the Lions were flying high into the merger of the AFL and NFL. It's just not occurred for the Detroit team since then.

They've had a season that saw them lose no games, and haven't played any playoff games since 1991 and have only made it to the playoffs 3 times since the beginning of the 21st century.

It's not looking like this season is likely to be any better than the last.

11. Philadelphia Eagles: 3 NFL titles as well as One Super Bowl Win

The Eagles had a solid period prior to the merger in 1967 and won a trio of titles in 1949, 1948, and 1960. In the years following the Eagles were virtually silent for more than 50 years. But, don't worry, the Eagles have won their first ever Super Bowl following the 2017 season, in which they won the game to a 13-3 win. This was far from a typical Super Bowl win for the Eagles however. In their regular seasons, the team's star player Carson Wentz played like one of the top footballers on the NFL. He ran for more than 3000 yards and scored 33 touchdowns and just seven interceptions. Just before the playoffs began however, he became injured and had to miss the remainder of the year. But don't fret it was a matter of time before an alternate player Nick Foles stepped into the position of the starter and led his fellow Eagles to their first Super Bowl win.

With the help of leading tight end Zach Ertz offensively and a defensively stingy one and a stingy defense, the Eagles managed to sneak over their opponents the Falcons in the opening round of the playoffs. They would beat the Vikings and then squeeze out a victory against Tom Brady and the Patriots in the Super Bowl.

It's been an interesting ride since then.

10. Cleveland Browns: 4 NFL Titles

The Browns might be considered to be the laughing stock of the present NFL However, the Browns were once during the 1950s, that the Browns were among the top teams. They took home NFL championships in 1950, 1954 1955 and

1964, which was just three years prior to the merger. For the Browns 1964 was their last year in which they considered winning the title. The Browns have been to the playoffs only 15 times since their merger, with 12 of them occurring prior to 1990.

While Browns supporters are enthusiastic as they get however their performance at the football field usually left much to be left to be desired. The Browns were in a position to play to in the Super Bowl last year but fell to Chiefs Chiefs at the end of the first round playoffs.

9. Indianapolis Colts: 3 NFL Titles and Two Super Bowl Wins

The Colts were awarded three NFL championships in their time as their team the Baltimore Colts in 1958, 1959 and 1968. They followed up their win in 1968 with one of the very first Super Bowls in the year 1971. In a memorable season which they went 11-2-1, the Colts had a solid record in both areas of field. The elder Johnny Unitas was the quarterback for the team. Even though the season wasn't his greatest year in stats, he played big when it was needed.

144

A second Super Bowl win wouldn't come in 2006 for one of the top offensive squads of NFL history. While the defense was mediocre, Hall of Fame Quarterback Peyton Manning and Hall of Fame Coach Tony Dungy led a fearsome offense to a 12-4 regular season record, before sweeping all of the Chiefs, Ravens, Patriots and Colts on their way to the Super Bowl victory.

Manning was phenomenal this season, throwing more than 4,000 yards, and finishing with 31 scores. Top receiving duo Marvin Harrison and Reggie Wayne were almost impossible to stop defensively.

Although they Colts have been solid since, they have not yet found the edge that will take their team to the next step.

8. San Francisco 49ers: 5 Super Bowl Wins

The San Francisco 49ers have been one of the most powerful teams since the merger between the AFL and NFL in 1967. They won five championships between 1982 and 1995 the team built a history of dominance by winning against other excellent franchises like The Miami Dolphins and Denver Broncos.

The first ring was awarded in 1981, when legendary coach Bill Walsh was able to get past Cincinnati's Cincinnati Bengals by a score of 26-21. With the help of famous football player Joe Montana and receiver Eddie Clark The 49ers were able ride an impressive offense over an aggressive Cincinnati team. The defense which was headed by Ronnie Lott, was also excellent.

In 1983 the team was better, with an impressive 15-1 record in the hands of Walsh along with Montana. Thanks to the Running back Wendell Tyler, the 1983 49ers defeated their opponents the Miami Dolphins in the Super Bowl and earned the team the second Super Bowl ring.

The next ring followed in 1988. The next occasion, Joe Montana teamed up with the star run-back Roger Craig and star wide receiver Jerry Rice to form one of the most dangerous trios that the entire league has ever seen. The offense was unstoppable and the 49ers yet again beat the Bengals with the total of 20-16.

Ring four followed in the year following with the same team. Joe Montana was awesome and Jerry Rice kept on improving.

146

The last ring was awarded in 1994. Joe Montana had retired but was replaced by a famous quarterback in Steve Young. With his legs and arm, Young was a star on the rise. Naturally, it was helpful to have a powerful Jerry Rice.

The 49ers returned to winning the Super Bowl in 2019, but have had a difficult few years since.

7. Dallas Cowboys: 5 Super Bowl Wins

The team from America The Cowboys were dominant during the period from 1993 until the year 1996. They took home three championships in the time frame, and added to the two titles they had already that they won in 1972 and in 1978.

This team from 1971, coached by the legendary Coach Tom Landry and quarterback Roger Staubach They were the very first Cowboys team to secure an Super Bowl victory, defeating the Dolphins by 24-3.

Their second Super Bowl, again under Tom Landry, came in 1978 when they racked up a 27-10 defeat by their opponents, the Denver Broncos. An offensive force that was dominant under the leadership of Staubach and also boasted an elusive 1,000-yard rusher who was Tony Dorsett.

After a brief time of poor performance after which the Cowboys were back on high in 1992. but this time under the direction of Hall of Famers Jimmy Johnson. The team finished with a 13-3 record during the season, and one of the top offensive teams in the game and the Cowboys depended on Hall of Fame quarterback Troy Aikman, running back Emmitt Smith, as well as player Michael Irvin. They were nearly impossible to stop which was the situation when the team swept Buffalo Bills 52-17 at the Super Bowl.

The second title came following year, the team cruising to a second Super Bowl win over the Bills and this time more competitive with their score at 30-13.

The Final Super Bowl came in 1995 in which they defeated the Steelers with the score of 27-17. It would be Aikman, Smith, and Irvin's last Super Bowl win, a trio that would be remembered in the history books as being among the most dominant sports teams has ever witnessed.

6. New England Patriots: 6 Super Bowl Wins

In the event that San Francisco 49ers were dominant and dominant, their counterparts in the New England Patriots were even superior. They are currently tied with the Pittsburgh Steelers for most Super Bowl wins, with six and counting, the Patriots hold the unique achievement of winning every one of them during the 20th century. A legendary team consisting with Head Coach Bill Belichick and quarterback Tom Brady will take care of that for you.

The Patriots have their own championship wins, including them, as well as the Rams (2002 as well as 2019), Panthers (2004), Eagles (2005), Seahawks (2015) as well as Seahawks (2015), and the Falcons (2017). Tom Brady has the most individual titles of all time having won seven (six with the Patriots and one with the Bucs).

What was the thing that made the Patriots dominance so thrilling to witness was the fact the fact that they were able to do it at both ends. Brady is certainly one of the greatest offensive players ever, no doubt however, Belichick is also among the greatest defensive minds ever. The deadly pair consisting of Belichick and Brady destroyed many teams' hopes of winning an NFL title between 2002 and 2019. After the duo split two years ago the Patriots haven't made the playoffs and are playing in 2021 in a non-fantastic football situation.

5. Washington Football Team Washington Football Team Championships in NFL, and 3 Super Bowls

It doesn't get any more balanced than this! Washington Football Team Washington Football Team has 3 NFL titles in their records and three Super Bowl wins, as well.

They debut Super Bowl win came in 1982, during a shorter NFL season. The team went 8-1 and managed to defeat their opponents Lions, Vikings, Cowboys and Dolphins on the way to their first ever Super Bowl. The team was led by player Joe Theismann and receiver Charlie Brown on offense, the team relied on its defense to win the trophy. The defense was helmed by the safety Tony Peters.

The next time they won the title was in 1987, but this time beating they defeated the Denver

Broncos by a lopsided score of 42-10. The group was spearheaded by the dominant wide receiver Gary Clark on offense and cornerback Barry Wilburn on defense.

Then, Washington was able to win the third championship in 1991, beating Buffalo Bills Buffalo Bills by a score of 37-24. The team was dominant. QB Mark Rypien had an awesome season on offense, along with the running back Ernest Byner and receiver Gary Clark. On the defensive side it was defensive lineman Darrell Green leading the way for Washington.

Washington hasn't been able to make it to the top of the league throughout the twenty-first century. They have made playoffs just two times over the past six seasons.

4. Pittsburgh Steelers: 6 Super Bowl Victories

The Steelers have been a top football team within the NFL over the course of many years. One of the teams that is most balanced teams in regards to Super Bowl victories, the Steelers had the chance to win four championships between 1975 and 1980, an impressive stretch that gave to the NFL public to "Steel Curtain," the name of their most dominant defensive line in this period of. After a period of silence for the bulk of the 1980s and 90s but the Steelers returned in a major manner in the 20th century, winning titles in the years 2005 and 2008.

The 2005 edition of the Steelers scored 11-5, beating an incredibly strong Indianapolis team as well as a Seattle Seahawks team to win their first Super Bowl of the 21st century. Coached by legend Bill Cowher, young quarterback Ben Roethlisberger, and running back Willie Parker, the Steelers were able to defeat Seattle in a tight game. On defense, the team had one of the greatest safety players ever: Troy Polamalu.

In 2008, the Pittsburgh Steelers and the 2008 Arizona Cardinals met in one of the most tense Super Bowl games of all time. It ended up being 27-22 with the Steelers barely escaping the frightened Cardinals. Ben Roethlisberger once again led the way for Pittsburgh and Santonio Holmes making the dramatic touchdown catch that won the game. On defense the team was led by Polamalu and the linebacker James Harrison creating trouble.

The Steelers haven't played in an Super Bowl in a while however, they are among the top reliable team that play in the NFL. It's a shock that Pittsburgh isn't in the playoffs!

3. Chicago Bears: 7 NFL Titles 1 Super Bowl

The Chicago Bears, one of the teams with the longest history in the NFL were a force before the merger and won an astonishing seven NFL titles prior to 1967. In Chicago it's always been focused on defense. The defense is strong, tough, and is likely to force you off the field when you are too close!

The only Super Bowl win came in 1985 by one of the most powerful teams of NFL history. In the regular season, with a an overall record of 15-1 The Bears beat all of the Giants and Rams in the playoffs prior to playing them and the Patriots at the Super Bowl. You know what? They took on the Patriots also and hammered the weak New England team with the score of 46-10. The 1985 Bears might have had the most effective defense in the history of football with head coach Mike Ditka. On offense, Jim McMahon was reliable and Hall of Hall of Famer Walter Payton was excellent, however, most importantly, it was defense, led by defensive linemen Richard Dent, defensive tackle Steve McMichael along with William "The The Refrigerator" Perry that struck fear in opponents. This team was brutal.

The Bears have played a great defense since the beginning of time--it's become a norm for them. However, they've been searching for an outstanding quarterback for many years.

2. New York Giants: 4 NFL Championships and 4, Super Bowl Wins

(Courtesy from unsplash.com.)

The New York Giants were originally named (in part) because of the huge towers that are located within New York City.

Always has been something unique regarding the New York Giants. While they hold the second-highest number of championships of any team they're always the underdogs. They were awarded four NFL Championships during 1927, 1934 1938 and 1956. Then, they had to struggle for a while to build confidence and find their feet.

The foundation was finally laid in the year 1986, in the year that the 14-2 Giants defeated the Denver Broncos to win their first ever Super Bowl by a score of 39-20. The team was coached by the legendary Coach Bill Parcells, quarterback Phil Simms and superstar player Joe Morris. The team also featured an outstanding defense, with defensive lineman Lawrence Taylor, one of the top linebackers in the history of football.

The following title was won three years later, in the year 1990. With the team again led by Parcells Parcells' Giants managed to move past the aggressive Buffalo Bills by a score of 20-19 in the championship match. Phil Simms won his second championship while the team was and again, relying heavily on Taylor as well as the linebacker Pepper Johnson.

It took some time to get there, but it was a long time before the Giants came back to at the Super Bowl in 2007, and this time, they were faced with the daunting job of defeating the undefeated New England Patriots, a team many believed to be the greatest ever. The 10-6 Giants did not seem to be worried, instead coming up with a stunning defeat of the Patriots with 17-14. The

Giants were driven by QB Eli Manning, receiver Plaxico Burress, and a solid defense. The game featured some of the more famous catch ever made of David Tyree.

The team would make it back to it's Super Bowl in 2011, with a similar record of 9-7, and had to defeat powerhouses such as The Green Bay Packers and San Francisco 49ers in order to have a shot. They were given the chance and this time it was Eli Manning leading the way against Tom Brady and the stacked New England Patriots. The top players Victor Cruz and Hakeem Nicks were the most effective offensive weapons, while defensive tackle Jason Pierre-Paul making destruction on defense. The game was another one that was close and the Giants defeated the Patriots in the second half, this time with the score of 21-17. It's tough enough for a team to take on Tom Brady and the Patriots when you're in the Super Bowl...the Giants were able to beat them twice!

Their luck has been slipping since that time, since the Giants haven't been to the playoffs since 2016, after they lost a game against the Packers.

1. Green Bay Packers: 9 NFL titles as well as Four Super Bowl Wins

The most dominant team of all time in NFL time is the small squad that hails from Green Bay, and it's not even that close. The fact that they have several of the best and most famous coaches in the history of football helps however However, Green Bay's continued dominance throughout its long time span is truly remarkable.

With an impressive nine NFL championships The Packers were easily their most successful team during the years prior to the merger of AFL and NFL.

When the two teams merged when they merged, the Packers have not slowed down at all. Their first win was in the very first Super Bowl in 1966. The legendary coach Vince Lombardi -- who was the Super Bowl trophy has since been named after--the 1966 Packers defeated the Chiefs with a crushing score of 35-10, claiming the first trophy ever. The team of Lombardi was 12-2 during the regular season before beating teams like the Cowboys as well as the Chiefs during the postseason. The squad was led by the legendary football player Bart Starr and a defense that was ranked among the top in the league across all areas.

The Packers returned next year to triumph again by beating their opponents the Oakland Raiders by a score of 33-14 in the 1967 Super Bowl. Lombardi won another title as the team's defense was just as impressive as ever.

It would take a time before the Packers returned to their "promised place." They took nearly three decades to be exact, however, they eventually found their way back in. In a game with the New England Patriots for the title and the title, the Packers defeated the Pats with 35-21. The team was well-equipped both on offense and defense This version of the Packers was led by the star football player Brett Favre. Defensively, safety LeRoy Butler was the main player, and defensive tackle Reggie White making it hard on quarterbacks, too.

It would be another decade until Green Bay would win another Super Bowl, this time under the leadership of star the quarterback Aaron Rodgers in 2010. The route towards winning the

Super Bowl wasn't easy, due to the Packers needing to eliminate their Eagles, Falcons, and Bears in order to take on an extremely strong Steelers team. The game was a close one but the Packers defeated the Steelers with 31-25. Rodgers was the most impressive player however the receiver Greg Jennings had an awesome season as well. On defense there was cornerback Charles Woodson and linebacker Clay Matthews who were a challenge for the opposing offensive teams.

The Green Bay Packers may be the most consistently successful squad of all time in NFL history. While they haven't been able to make an appearance in the Super Bowl game since 2010 The Packers are expected to be in the playoffs each season. Since the beginning of the 21st century there has been just few seasons during which the Packers did not make the playoffs. With a fervent fan base with a fantastic player with the name of Aaron Rodgers, and a unique home-field advantage in Lambeau Field, the legendary Lambeau Field, the entirety of the Packers team is exactly the same as legendary.

Chapter 6: The Top Players In All Time

After we've discussed the most successful franchises in history now it's time to take a look at the top players of the past. The task of selecting the best players in a sport such as football is a lot more difficult than choosing the best players for soccer or basketball. Why? because the NFL is split into three distinct areas of the game. There's the offense, defense, and then there are special teams. There is no aspect of the game that is "more crucial" than the others and so deciding on a top player in all three aspects of the game can be quite difficult. Consider the NBA for instance, where each participant on court has to play defense and offense simultaneously. The NFL has established positions for defense and offense!

It is possible to go step-by-step and look at the most effective ways to do it. That's exactly what we're going to discuss during this section. From the most flashy quarterbacks, to the most grittiest offensive linemen This chapter will take an in-depth look at each position and identify

160

some of the top players to put on the top chinstrap! I hope that you're as thrilled like I am.

The Best players in the World of All Time at Each Position

Quarterback: It's only appropriate to begin by playing the position with the most attention. In not in any particular order, here are the best quarterbacks ever to play the game.

Troy Aikman (1989-2000) Played for the Dallas Cowboys: Compared to other players listed, Troy Aikman may seem to be an odd choice. Why? It's because there wasn't anything Aikman did that was especially extravagant, especially when compared with his fellow teammates Emmitt Smith or Michael Irvin. Aikman was often compared to the two players. Smith as well as Irvin have both been named Hall of Famer who were among the top at what a running-back and receiver pair could provide. Therefore Aikman, the head of the Cowboys during this time, Aikman, probably didn't receive the respect he merited. This seems a bit cheap due to the fact that the things Aikman performed in playing field, as a player and leader placed him among the top to ever perform at the position of quarterback. He was composed, calm and cool. All qualities you look for in a quarterback. While his statistics aren't anywhere near as impressive as Tom Brady or Peyton Manning, Aikman was still able to lead his Cowboys to three Super Bowl victories in just 11 seasons. He was precise when he played the ball and made smart choices and nearly always put his team in position to possibly beat the opposition in football. Like most great players, He seemed to play his most assured football in the moments that mattered the most. He finished three-for-three at the Super Bowl and threw a total of five touchdowns, and only one interception during the three games.

Joe Montana (1979-1994) Played for the San Francisco 49ers and Kansas City Chiefs: Joe Montana was unique because he was always able to be at his best in the moments that mattered most. He was the proud owner of 4 Super Bowl trophies and three Super Bowl Most Valuable Player (MVP) awards, Montana shone the brightest when the lights were on. Also, he has the amazing accomplishment of not losing in a Super Bowl game (4-0). The model for all players who want to be a part of the NFL cool Joe was an exceptional talent. Another interesting fact about Joe was that he was the player that Tom Brady idolized growing up. If Montana was not as exceptional a player, perhaps the NFL world wouldn't have been gifted with the talent from Tom Brady...something to consider!

Otto Graham (1946-1955) Played for the Cleveland Browns: One of the legends that are not known to have played the game. Otto Graham was a three-time NFL champion for the Browns during the late 1940s from the mid-1950s. A quarterback who completely changed the game through his blend of passing and running Graham is considered to be one of the most famous Cleveland Browns in NFL history. Graham was inducted into the Hall of Fame in 1965 and was a five-time professional bowler. It is important to note that The Pro Bowl is something that occurs every year and is a chance for the top players in the regular season of every team to play for the title of the All-Star Game. It is considered to be a prestigious honour, but it is not as great as being on the Hall of Fame!

Peyton Manning (1998-2015) Played for the Indianapolis Colts and Denver Broncos Tom

Brady's greatest rivals Peyton Manning was a phenomenal quarterback who put together some of the most impressive statistics of all time. Additionally Manning also won two Super Bowls as well as five MVPs and holds numerous records for touchdowns, passing yards and other awards. Most likely, his greatest achievement came in 2013 when he was a part of his team, the Denver Broncos. In 2013, he was able to throw for 55 touchdowns and nearly 5500 yards! These numbers are truly amazing and average over three touchdowns per game!

Johnny Unitas (1955-1973) Played for the Pittsburgh Steelers, Baltimore Colts and San Diego Chargers: Another Colts quarterback makes an appearance here. The Hall of Fame quarterback and four-time NFL champion, Johnny Unitas helped open the way for Troy Aikman's and Peyton Maning's and Troy Aikman's of the NFL. With the title "the Golden Arm," it's not surprising that Unitas was able to hold the record for the most games that had a touchdown pass before it was broken in 2012 by Drew Brees in 2012. The record stood for more than 50 years! The most fundamental strong, tough and extremely skilled, Unitas is considered by many to be the very first great quarterback.

While he is no longer a player with his former team, the New England Patriots, Tom Brady will always be remembered as an iconic Boston legend. Tom Brady is among the most loved players throughout the history of the sport-rich city even though he currently is a part of Tampa Bay Buccaneers. Tampa Bay Buccaneers.

Tom Brady (2000-Present) Played for the New England Patriots and Tampa Bay Buccaneers I know I mentioned that this list would be in no specific order, but there's an argument for that explains why Tom Brady is going last in the quarterbacks. Tom Brady is arguably the Greatest quarterback of All Time at the position and has won many Super Bowls (7) than any other team (NFL titles not included). These are truly amazing numbers. The most shocking aspect? Brady continues to do the same thing in the present. In spite of being in the NFL for more than 20 years, Brady has been ranked as the leader in the whole NFL by passing yards as of the date of this publication. Although he's certainly been surrounded by outstanding players, coaches and defenses during his time, it does not change his status as Brady is the most successful quarterback of all time. He's three times MVP and a 13-time Pro-Bowler. The man is unstoppable . He'll be admitted into the Hall of Fame shortly after the time he retires.

Running Backs:

Barry Sanders (1989-1998) Played for the Detroit Lions: Another running back with a short time in the game, Barry Sanders was one of the most exciting players to ever walk onto the football field. Some consider him the greatest player not to play in the Super Bowl, Sanders still received one league MVP award and four appearances in the Pro Bowl, and a Hall of Fame induction in 2004. While he wasn't a large or powerful player, Sanders used incredible speed and footwork as well as the ability to maneuver around, over the air, and even through defenders! In the entire 10 seasons Sanders played the game, he was always a rusher of 1,000 yards. Simply put it was a once-in-a-generation talent.

Emmitt Smith (1990-2004) was a player in his team, the Dallas Cowboys: Even with other Hall of

Famer Troy Aikman and Michael Irvin taking his touches away, Emmitt Smith was still an undisputed force in the Dallas Cowboys offense for over 10 years. He was the recipient of the MVP award, a Super Bowl MVP, and an induction into the Hall of Fame, Emmitt Smith was almost unstoppable on an outstanding Cowboys offensive line. His greatest season was 1995, when he ran for more than 1,700 yards, adding over 350 more receiving yards, and was responsible for 25 touchdowns! These numbers are impressive, as was Emmitt...he is among the top running backs ever to play the game.

Walter Payton (1975-1987) Played for the Chicago Bears The Chicago Bears: While Gale Sayers may have set the scene for some incredible Chicago run-backs Walter Payton took the idea and ran with it -- literally! He's among the most reliable running backs ever, securing his place in the Hall of Fame, while being awarded MVP and a Super Bowl MVP trophy, as well. The best year he had was in 1977, when he racked up for more than 1,800 yards and had 20 touchdowns. Strong, slick and fast and tough, it took an entire army to bring him down when he was in the field. A man as good on playing as in the game, the NFL ultimately established the Walter Payton Man of the Year Award. It is considered to be one of the most prestigious awards in the NFL It is given to an athlete who has shown exceptional service outside of the field.

Jim Brown (1957-1965) Played for the Cleveland Browns: Much like Tom Brady and the list of quarterbacks, although I said that the list was not in any specific order, it's fairly evident it is that Jim Brown is the best running back ever to play the game. He's a Hall-of-Fame winner who was a winner of the Super Bowl, was a three-time MVP, and was one of the toughest athletes to wear the NFL jersey. His most memorable season was 1963, when he scored more than 2,000 yards of all-purpose and scored 15 touchdowns. He was more powerful than every other player ever to play this position and also with speed, Jim Brown is one of the very few players in NFL time that can be certain that he will be capable of dominating regardless of the time period that he played in.
Wide Receiver:

Randy Moss (1998-2012): played with the Minnesota Vikings, Oakland Raiders, New England Patriots, Tennessee Titans, and San Francisco

49ers Although Jerry Rice is likely the most impressive wide receiver ever to play, Randy Moss wasn't far from the top. I'll not forget the season when Tom Brady together with Tom Brady teamed up back in 2007. While he was able to have more statistically impressive seasons prior to his time as a player with his team, the Minnesota Vikings, his career revival with his team the New England Patriots was simply remarkable to see. He scored 22 (!) touchdowns, and nearly 1,500 yards of receiving for the Patriots during the season. Randy Moss as well as Brady could not be stopped. After winning the Super Bowl and being inducted into the Hall of Fame a few years after, Randy Moss will forever be among the most talented receivers ever to perform the position.

Jerry Rice (1985-2004): He played in the San Francisco 49ers, Oakland Raiders and the Seattle Seahawks: Considered by many as the second-best offensive player ever, Jerry Rice won an astonishing three Super Bowls along with his quarterback Joe Montana, for the San Francisco 49ers. Jerry Rice had some of the most memorable seasons as a member of the 49ers as well as his best especially in 1995. In 1995, he racked up more than 1,800 receiving yards in addition to 15 touchdowns. He was big, consistent and tough beyond any doubt, Jerry Rice was near impossible to guard, no matter if he was playing alongside Montana as well as any of the other quarterbacks. He was simply a rare talent.

Tight End:

Tony Gonalez (1997-2013): He played in The Kansas City Chiefs and Atlanta Falcons The greatest tight end ever is definitely Tony Gonzalez. A superb blocker, pass-catcher and runner of the football field, Gonzales almost unstoppable. He played a huge role in introducing a brand new kind of tight end in the field. Prior to Gonzalez tight ends, tight ends were primarily blocking players, but only a little. They could occasionally take a catch, yes but their primary priority was opening up the lane for running backs to move through. Gonzalez altered the way they did that. His most memorable season was in 2000 when he was a part of the Kansas City Chiefs. In that season, he racked up more than 1,200 yards, and scored nine touchdowns. Prior to him, these figures were only seen at wide receivers! A superb player in as well off of the field Gonzalez is inducted in the Hall of Fame in 2019. Despite not winning an Super Bowl, Gonzalez remains one of the top players to ever play at the position of tight end.

Offensive Line:

Forrest Gregg (1956-1971) Played for the Green Bay Packers and Dallas Cowboys While offensive linemen don't receive the same respect like the other offensive players performing any offensive activity without these massive bodies protecting your quarterback is impossible. Forrest Gregg, a Hall of Famer, and a fixture on Vince Lombardi's Super bowl-winning teams, was an excellent player as both a pass protector as well as a run blocker. Gregg won eight championships that spanned through the pre-merger period until the beginning of the 70s. If you are counting at home...yes! This is greater than Tom Brady has won.

Defense

Linebacker:

Lawrence Taylor (1981-1993) Played for the New York Giants: Not just the New York Giants' Lawrence Taylor the greatest linebacker ever and he's probably the most effective defensive player ever. In the spirit of "defense is the key to winning championships," Taylor was one of the most formidable players to play during the entire history of football. Quick, powerful and tough Taylor made it hard for offensive lineman to take the chance to compete against him. He was the winner of two championships for the Giants but his best season probably coming in 1986, when he successful in accumulating 20.5 sacks! Although the half-sack statistic might seem odd to certain people however, it's crucial to remember that players are able to split sacks when they both arrive at the quarterback. The most likely hard-hitting player of all time, Lawrence Taylor was one player you would not wish to cross.

Defensive End:

Reggie White (1985-2000) Played for the Philadelphia Eagles, Green Bay Packers and the Carolina Panthers: Another player who excelled at going after quarterbacks Many consider Reggie White to be the most effective pass-rusher of all

172

time. In such a tense position, you need a certain kind of strength to endure the everyday grind and to pursue the quarterback. This is Reggie White. Inexhaustible, quick and strong, Reggie White was able to beat nearly any lineman and modify the plan of the quarterback. His most successful season was 1987, when he managed to register 21.0 tackles in the Philadelphia Eagles. He was a Super Bowl champion, defensive player of the year as well as a Hall of Famer Reggie White was able to complete the feat throughout his 14-year career.

Defensive Tackle

Joe Greene (1969-1981) Played for the Pittsburgh Steelers: Anybody with the name "Mean" Joe Greene has been considered to be one of the top defensive players of all time, isn't it? With Joe Greene's case...yes! Four-time Super Bowl champion with the Pittsburgh Steelers, Joe Green established the foundation for the incredible lineup of defensive lines in Pittsburgh. In terms of his role Joe Green was the primary reason for the Steelers nickname during those years"The Steel Curtain. The best of his seasons was likely in 1972 when he capable of registering 11 sacks in addition to being among the most feared run stoppers within the NFL. An unquestionably Hall of Famer and a brutal opponent, Joe Greene helped pave the way for today's defensive tackle.

Safety:

Ronnie Lott (1981-1994) Played for the San Francisco 49ers, Los Angeles Raiders and New York Jets: Another four-time Super Bowl champion, Ronnie Lott was able to leave his mark in the league by being a shrewd player, a good defensive player on the perimeter, and an excellent leader. Although Joe Montana was the focal player on offensive, Lott was holding down the defensive fort. He was a Hall of Famers, and many believe Lott to be one of the most reliable security of all time. I'm having a difficult time being adamant!

Cornerback:

Deion Sanders (1989-2000 Deion Sanders (1989-2000, 2004-2005) was a player in The Atlanta Falcons, San Francisco 49ers, Dallas Cowboys, Washington Redskins, and Baltimore Ravens Prior to when Deion Sanders came to the scene the cornerback position not exactly glamorous. There were many who mocked the position and claimed it was for the who couldn't even make it as an athlete! However, Deion "Primetime" Sanders has changed that perception. Quick, powerful and unstoppable, Deion Sanders was able to fend off receivers, while being among the best kick-returners of NFL history. Once the ball was placed in Sanders' hands, he proved virtually impossible to stop because of his combination of speed and elusiveness. In the modern NFL cornerbacks aren't less respected than they were prior to when Sanders entered the field. Sanders is a two-time Super Bowl champion and a Hall of Inductee.

Chapter 7: Top Nfl Coaches Of All Time

Although it could appear that the job of the coach isn't all that important when we've spent all day talking about players, it couldn't be more wrong. The coach performs a myriad of responsibilities that are part of each NFL game. They need to communicate with their players to develop strategies to prepare the opponent, devise innovative play ideas to lead their team along the field as well as balance the egos and personalities of their players and many more. In the absence of a head coach the entire procedure would collapse.

What is the best coach? The truth of the thing is that there's no one perfect model. A coach such as Jimmy Johnson, for example is well-known for his excellent relationship with his players as well as being friendly with his players. Bill Belichick, on the contrary, is robust as they come, and is more focused on the aspects of strategy and the culture.

In this section we will examine the top 10 coaches ever to play from the NFL. To compile this list, we'll be sorting them out in order, unlike the best players in every position!

The Top 10 Most Outstanding Coaches in NFL History

10. Bill Parcells

In the top 10 spots in the rankings, we also have Bill Parcells, nicknamed "Big Tuna." As a coach for 19 years with four different teams, Parcells was able to win two Super Bowls during his time as a player for The New York Giants. He had a record of 172-130 overall (11-8 in playoffs), Parcells is possibly best known as the coach of Bill Belichick (we will hear more about him in the near future). But more than that, Parcells was a calm clever, intelligent, and powerful player on the sidelines who could convey much while saying little. His teams were renowned for their toughness when it came to defense. This was aided by the fact that the team had Lawrence Taylor on his Giants teams for the two seasons the team won Super Bowls. the team.

9. Chuck Noll

The Steelers weren't always the dominating team that we have come to admire over the decades. Prior to the time that Chuck Noll arrived, in fact, they had not won an Super Bowl in over 35 years. When Chuck Noll arrived and they won four times over the course of six seasons. The Hall of Famers with a dazzling record in the playoffs of 16-8, Chuck Noll epitomized what it meant to be part of the Steelers team. He was loud, tough and abrasive however he loved his players very much. The Steelers have had amazing coaches such as Bill Cowher and Mike Tomlin however none has been able to match the successes which Chuck Noll brought to the team.

8. Tom Landry

Very few coach were as steady in their commitment to excellence than Tom Landry. Landry had a successful 29 seasons , and was averaging 20 consecutive seasons which included winning seasons. Add to this his impressive 20-16 performance in the playoffs and you've got yourself a legendary Dallas Cowboys head coach. Slick, cool, and hard on the sidelines with your players. You could see that Landry was a master of his teams and their decisions. When you look at the top coaches ever there is no list that doesn't include Landry appearing.

7. George Halas

One of the most successful coaching staffs of all time in NFL the past, George Halas coached the Bears -- the "Monsters from the Midway"--for forty seasons. If he was a coach in the current NFL and had his name included on this list could be more prominent. However, Halas was able to accumulate more than 300 wins as well as six NFL titles and an entry into the Hall of Fame directly after the time he retired. The Chicago Bears have always been known for their strong, hard-nosed and physically-based football. Halas best embodied these values than other coaches in long-running team's past.

6. Joe Gibbs

A legend among legends Joe Gibbs won three Super Bowls as a quarterback with three different players during his time at Washington. A legacy built by his incredible defensive play, Gibbs was consistent, solid and reliable in the backfield with the Redskins. A warm and friendly person, Joe Gibbs was able to guide his teams with a mixture of kindness and hard-hitting when the time was right. With a record of 154-94 overall and a 17-7 record in playoffs, Gibbs was one coach who was deserving of more respect because of what he did for Washington.

5. Paul Brown

The person behind the name, you've had an impact when you've got an entire company called after you (the Cleveland Browns). The winner of seven championships and an honorary Hall of Famer at the age of 1967. Paul Brown will forever be remembered as one of the top pioneers and coaches of NFL history. One of the most remarkable facts I can offer regarding Paul Brown is that he was able to participate in ten consecutive championship game (!) during the period 1946-56. The overall score of 213-104 is sure to be remembered in history as among the greatest in the history of football.

4. Bill Walsh

When you think of the current NFL offense and the way it was created then take a look at 49ers's head coach Bill Walsh. From 1979 until 1988, as a coach, Walsh was able to make the switch from a run-heavy plan to a more pass-oriented one through the introduction of remarkable players like Joe Montana and Jerry Rice into his offensive. The winner of four Super Bowls (4-0), Walsh will forever be known as Joe Montana's second-half coach. He was cool, fun, and friendly, but he was also not afraid to take on anyone who made mistakes. A record that was 92-59 overall as well as an overall record in the playoffs of 10-4, Walsh was one of the most successful postseason coaches of NFL time.

Conclusion

This is the conclusion of our journey. I hope that you loved the book and had a blast discovering the fascinating background of NFL football. It concludes with some inspiring stories and interesting information about the game I , along with many others love so much.

What I was trying to convey through this book is that football has an unfair image. Although it is an extremely violent game that can result in injury to many players however this is not enough to eliminate it as a game that is only performed by violent players.

From the lives from Tom Brady to Doug Baldwin to Michael Oher, I wanted to make clear that these were individuals, just like us. People who put in a lot of effort to get to where they came to.

Football was created in the 19th century, because there was something in the idea of combining soccer and rugby into an entirely American game that was embraced by the majority of people. Although baseball is the American pastime but the game of football represents America as it is in the purest sense: We are resilient, tough physical, and affectionate with our team members. This is football. This is what we grew up to learn and that's what I hope that you will take away from this book.

Additionally, I am hoping that you have gained more information about the game. While the foundation of football is a simple concept in terms of ideology, the fact of the thing is that there's numerous aspects that make up your typical football team. If you're an observer, coach or special teams player offensive or defensive player it is an all-team sport, straightforward and easy. There is no way to be a weak link when you are hoping to play to the NFL. One weak link is transformed into several weak links, which transform into a poor football team.

While I wouldn't want anyone who had no knowledge of the game to become an expert on the game I do hope you are aware of the amount of effort, time and rules go into football. It's not an unforgiving game instead, it's a contest of geniuses competing to beat each other!

At the start of my book set out a scenario where there was a soccer match and you were completely confused in what was happening at the time. I would like to ensure that next time you watch the game, you're not just following the game, but even offering tips to your loved ones and friends!

If you're not successful do not forget the interesting facts...they were designed to impress.

Printed in the USA
CPSIA information can be obtained
at www.ICGtesting.com
LVHW020748070923
757423LV00009B/383